"*The Gospel According to Broadway* isn't quite an evangelistic treatise using various Broadway shows to explicate the gospel, unless one understands that the root word *euangelion* literally means "good news." Indeed, the book is full of good news, the good news of God's love for humanity and desire to be in relationship with us, despite all our foibles. Carter lays sacred texts from every biblical genre—books of law, history, poetry, wisdom literature, prophetic literature, the Gospels, and letters—alongside well-known Broadway productions in order for each to inform the other. Preachers looking for good sermon material will find Carter's book a useful resource, and others—without any agenda—will find it simply a good read."

—Robin Sandbothe, Pastor, Bethel Church, Columbia, Missouri
Associate, Pinnacle Leadership Associates; Coach

"Terrell Carter is one of the most creative people I know—pastor, theologian, educator, artist, social entrepreneur. He now brings his creative lens to *The Gospel According to Broadway*. This volume not only provides rich theological and biblical insights, but also encourages us to engage our culture as a means of communicating the gospel. Carter draws on Broadway shows (some more familiar than others) to share biblical truths that lead to a pointed application—sometimes with a bit of a twist. The reader will find the book both entertaining and inspirational."

—Ircel Harrison, Supplemental Professor of Missional Theology
Central Seminary, Shawnee, Kansas

"Terrell Carter's delightful book will send you back to the Bible for more reading and back to the theater (or TV screen) for more shows. Perfect for individuals or small group sessions, he takes familiar modern tales to help us reconsider the old stories that should guide our lives. Not only will you enjoy this book, but I doubt you'll make it through without humming some classic showtunes."

—Brian Kaylor, President and Editor-in-Chief, *Word & Way*

"Terrell Carter masterfully broadens the reader's understanding of what the full gospel of Christ entails. By creatively connecting the plots of various Broadway musicals to the greater story of God's movement, the reader begins to imagine a deeper life of resurrection. While reading *The Gospel According to Broadway*, I find myself at the intersection of 42nd Street and God's great story—and that is a truly sacred place."

—David McDaniel, Senior Pastor,
Holmeswood Baptist Church, Kansas City, Missouri

"People of faith can become so enmeshed in their scriptures that they forget they are reading a story with plot, characters, setting, and conflict. Sometimes the antidote to that amnesia is to set our holy texts alongside other stories to tease out the common elements. That is exactly what Terrell Carter has done here. He masterfully directs a production of the Bible's generative narrative alongside beloved tales of the stage. His words also illumine how our own stories intersect with God's grand story. Bravo, Terrell! Take a bow!"

—Tyler Tankersley, Senior Pastor, Ardmore Baptist Church
Winston-Salem, North Carolina

"Carter unpacks profound theological and biblical concepts, artistically connecting them with major themes from Broadway's greatest productions. Whether for personal reflection, biblical scholarship, or pastoral leadership, Carter offers an engaging and coherent work of art in *The Gospel According to Broadway*."

—Adam B. Banks, Pastor, First Baptist Church, Springfield, Ohio

THE GOSPEL
According to
BROADWAY

Terrell Carter

© 2021 Published in the United States
by Nurturing Faith, Macon, GA.

Nurturing Faith is a book imprint of
Good Faith Media (goodfaithmedia.org)
Library of Congress Cataloging-in-Publication
Data is available.

ISBN: 978-1-63528-161-3

All rights reserved. Printed in the
United States of America.

Scripture citations are taken from the
New Revised International Version (NRSV)
unless otherwise indicated

Cover and interior design by Amy C. Cook.
Cover concept by Benjamin H. Cook.
Cover photo by Andy Wilis on Unsplash. Motion blurred from original.

DEDICATION

To Rev. Dr. Warren Hoffman:
I learned more about preaching, creativity,
and pastoral care in the few years I served under your
leadership than I can ever repay. Thank you for taking
me under your wing and for being a friend.

*To the community at Central Baptist
Theological Seminary in Shawnee, Kansas:*
Thank you for helping me reevaluate my theology and beliefs
about God's kingdom and who can participate in it.

To the members of Webster Groves Baptist Church:
Thank you for being patient with me
as I continue to become the leader you need and want.

To Genevieve and Jerry Carter:
Thank you for life more abundant.

CONTENTS

ix
PREFACE

xiii
INTRODUCTION
What Is the Gospel?

1
ONE BIG FALLIBLE FAMILY
Joseph and the Amazing Technicolor Dreamcoat
Genesis 50:15-21

5
LOVE IS MORE THAN A FEELING
The Sound of Music
Ruth 1:8-18

11
THE VALUE OF AVOIDING EVIL INFLUENCES
The Producers
Psalm 1:1-6

15
CHOOSING WISDOM
The 25th Annual Putnam County Spelling Bee
Proverbs 1:1-7

19
(IN THE END) YOU CAN WIN
The Wiz
Ecclesiastes 1:12-18

25
RECONCILED FOR GOOD
Wicked
Matthew 5:21-26, 38-42

29
YOU DON'T HAVE TO WORRY
The Lion King
Matthew 6:25-34

35
LOVE, REGARDLESS
Rent
Luke 8:26-39

41
WE DON'T HAVE TO BE WORLDS APART
Big River
Acts 10:34-35

45
BE CAREFUL WHAT YOU FEED
Little Shop of Horrors
Romans 12:9-21

51
GO AND TELL THAT
Hairspray
1 Corinthians 12:12-14

57
LOVE IS HEALTHY
The Phantom of the Opera
1 Corinthians 13:1-8, 13

63
HARMONY AMID REAL LIFE
Mary Poppins
Philippians 2:1-11

69
WHERE'S YOUR YELLOW TICKET?
Les Miserables
James 2:1-9

75
CONCLUSION
The Gospel Revisited

PREFACE

Depending on who you ask, a good story contains between five and ten components that help readers understand what is happening, why they should care about the characters, and how the story will ultimately end. For this book, I have decided that five components are enough, and I have chosen to discuss the characters, setting, plot, conflict, and resolution only enough so as not to bore you! When combined creatively, the connections between these five components can keep the story running smoothly and allow readers to stay engaged to the end.

1. Characters: The individuals taking part in the action
2. Setting: The place or places where the action occurs
3. Plot: The main events of the story
4. Conflict: The struggle between characters that provides tension
5. Resolution: The solution to the conflict

The Bible tells God's story—the primary character is God, the Creator of all things.

The setting is primarily Earth because God's home is holy and unseeable and, as the writers of the Bible said, God is spirit and exists outside of everything that God created. To bridge the gap between God's invisibility and humankind's physicality, God created places such as the Garden of Eden, the Tabernacle, and Solomon's Temple as points where the holy and human could overlap.

The main plot of the story is that God values relationships. It seems as though God created all things—especially humankind—to be in relationship. All relationships are important: relationships between the holy and human; relationships between the human and human; and relationships between humans and the rest of created order. God created a world for humankind to live in and spaces within that world where God could interact with humans. God also created the world as a place for humankind to live among each other. God outlined God's expectations for what it means for humans to be in relationship with their Creator and with each other; indeed, humans are to recognize God's majesty and authority and to recognize and affirm the love and care that God wants for all people and creation. By setting these parameters, God helps humans understand that they can trust the One who created them, and that trust should influence not only their relationship with God but also with each other.

The conflict in the story is that humans disregarded the parameters God set for relationships. Instead of trusting that God loved them and had their best interests at heart, humankind doubted God and went against God's request. We learn that the first rebellion occurred in the Garden of Eden when humankind, instead of being thankful for what God had already provided for them and being satisfied with the work God had designated them to do, went after the one thing God told them was off limits. After this, God's relationship with humans changed. The Bible describes this mistrust and what came about from it as sin. God's holy character could not stand sin (the distrust that humans exhibited) and eventually removed humans from the space where the holy and human could reside together in uninterrupted relationship. Instead of living in perfection, humankind and all creation struggled.

After this first act of rebellion, God removed humankind from the Garden of Eden; humankind then rebelled in their relationships with each other. Instead of understanding that God had created the world for everyone, humankind began wanting what others had. More relationships were destroyed, more lives were damaged, and God's heart was further broken.

— PREFACE —

Since humankind's descent into sin, resolution has been hard to come by. What we learn in the early chapters of the Bible is that humankind continues to focus on gaining material wealth and controlling others instead of being in relationship with God and each other according to God's desires.

The Bible affirms humanity's unwillingness and inability to appreciate the opportunities God provided them. Yet, despite humanity's failures, God never gives up hope or turns away from the desire of people to restore relationships. God's faithfulness serves as the foundation of the "good news" that is the gospel.

INTRODUCTION
What Is the Gospel?

The Greek word for "gospel" is *euangelion*, which means "good news." At its core, the gospel is the good news of God's love. Although we primarily understand and interact with the word gospel as it relates to Jesus' life, death, and resurrection, it actually originated with the good news found in the early pages of the Hebrew Bible that, in spite of humankind's rebellion, God would not only remain in relationship with humanity but would also go even further by personally repairing the relationship between God and humankind. This endless love expressed by God toward humanity and all of creation is the essence of the gospel.

In Hebrews 10:4-10, the writer explores the intent and history of the process of how, in the beginning, God provided humankind with the means to participate in restored relationship with the Creator (by receiving forgiveness and being restored from sin) through a system of conciliatory sacrifices and how later Jesus, through his life, death, and resurrection, fulfilled God's intentions for an uninterrupted relationship with humankind.

Hebrews is a study in the contrasts of faithfulness, in particular God's faithfulness to be in relationship with humankind in contrast to humankind's inconsistent participation in that faithful relationship. We learn in Hebrews that God has always been consistent in actions and attitudes toward humankind. That consistency began in the Garden of Eden and continued through the covenant God made to Abraham to bless him with a family that would eventually bless the entire world.

God's covenant was reaffirmed to descendants of Abraham, including Jacob (later known as Israel), Moses, David, Solomon, and other prophets whom God used to remind humankind of God's promises to love, cherish, and be in relationship with them, no matter how far they strayed from their Creator. This inconsistent participation in relationship with God, whether by those leaders or by the people they led, was why a symbolic, sacrificial system was created early on in the Bible.

This sacrificial system was practiced on a daily, weekly, monthly, and yearly calendar, but it could not fully accomplish what God wanted for humankind: the full and complete transformation of humankind and restoration of relationships. Despite being God-ordained, the main thing the sacrificial system accomplished was to remind people of their sin (mistrust toward God).

People regularly participated in the processes of the sacrificial system because they regularly sinned against God and each other, but participation in the system was not conducive to feelings of joy: they felt pain and embarrassment for not being or doing as God wanted. This pain and embarrassment, however, did not always deter people from doing things that damaged their relationships with God and each other.

In response to their personal sin, they made offerings to God at the Temple—a place where the Hebrew people believed that God's space (God's presence) and the space of humankind overlapped, as originally occurred in the Garden of Eden. The sacrifices made at the Temple were symbolic compensation to God for the damage done to holy relationships by human sin. The sacrifices provided a symbolic purification for the community and made it possible for God to continue to dwell among unholy people.

This process was best understood through the Day of Atonement. During this annual communal ritual, people from the community went to the Temple to make sacrifices and to symbolically repent of their sins against God and each other. The Day of Atonement was different from other offering days, however, in that the priest would make a sacrifice on behalf of the entire community. A lamb would be killed, and its blood spread throughout the Temple.

— INTRODUCTION —

The blood was even spread in the most important room of the Temple: the Holy of Holies, the place where everyone believed God's tangible presence dwelled. The blood was spread as a way to symbolically cleanse the area. Another lamb, called a scapegoat, was then sent out from the Temple into the wilderness. This lamb symbolically carried the sins of the community away from the presence of God and the people. Thus the community was purified, and the people were cleansed, allowing them to have a relationship with God.

Although this ritual was ordained by God, the process was not perfect because humans continued to sin. As such, the Day of Atonement had to be repeated every year. Writing for The Bible Project, Tim Mackie and Aeron Sullivan explain the shortcomings of the ritual: "There was a deficiency of some kind, not in the ritual, but in the humans surrounding the temple! It was their sin that kept piling up year after year. What was needed was something that would purify not only the temple, but the corrupt and selfish human heart."[1]

The remedy for humanity's sin arrived in the form of Jesus Christ. It was the life, death, and resurrection of Jesus—the sinless Son of God—that came as the fulfillment of the sacrificial process. By coming into this world, living as he did, then dying and rising again by God's power, Jesus fulfilled the need of the sacrificial system. His life, death, and resurrection made it possible for God, the Holy One, to dwell among unholy people in a perfect way. Jesus proved to be the new space where God's space (presence) and human space overlapped. Through him, humankind was, and is, truly forgiven and restored to full relationship with God.

Our relationship with God was framed through sin and understood through the sacrificial system. Now, our relationship with God is framed through love and understood through Jesus' sacrifice. Through Jesus, our relationship with God is no longer based on a system, but through accepting and imitating the sacrificial acts Jesus exemplified through his life. Through Jesus' covering act, our relationship with God is complete. That is what the good news of the gospel is all about. It found its beginnings in God's love for what and who God created, and that love continued, even after humankind rebelled, and was ultimately fulfilled through Jesus.

In the preceding pages I have defined the good news of the gospel in a limited way, but will explore the components of this story more extensively through the words of the prophet Isaiah in the conclusion of this book. Until then, we will approach the gospel story through allusions to various Broadway plays as we explore the implications of God's love for all creation and how God's unwavering love should impact the way in which we live in relationship with our Creator, each other, and all that God has made.

Note

1 Tim Mackie and Aeron Sullivan, "Old Rituals and New Realities," https://bibleproject.com/blog/old-rituals-new-realities/ (accessed April 16, 2021).

ONE BIG FALLIBLE FAMILY

Joseph and the Amazing Technicolor Dreamcoat
Genesis 50:15-21

A well-traveled musical by Tim Rice and Andrew Lloyd Webber, *Joseph and the Amazing Technicolor Dreamcoat* is based on the life of the Old Testament character Joseph of whom we learn in Genesis 30–50. The musical provides a rousing and catchy look at Joseph's experiences of being the favorite son of Jacob, of falling into a pit by the hands of his brothers, and of rising to become the second-most important person in the land of Egypt.

It is challenging to look at familiar stories from the Bible that we learned as children because we struggle to reread them or interact with them with the patience and care of an adult to see if God's spirit can shed new light on them. The story of Joseph is one such example.

It begins under circumstances most of us would find less than appealing: Jacob has fallen in love with a young woman named Rachel and has asked her father, Laban, for her hand in marriage. Laban agrees but requires Jacob to work for him for seven years to be able to marry Rachel. After the seven-year contract is fulfilled, Laban throws a lavish wedding ceremony, and Jacob is happy to be marrying the woman of his dreams. The following morning, however, Jacob discovers that he has not married Rachel, the love of his life, but instead has been tricked by Laban into marrying Rachel's older sister Leah, who is not as physically appealing as Rachel. When Jacob confronts Laban about his trickery, he ends up agreeing to work an additional seven years to be able to marry Rachel. Not only is this troublesome for Jacob, but the two sisters also do not take well to this decision.

The sisters eventually begin to compete for Jacob's affections. For a long time Leah, the less desirable sister, holds the advantage over Rachel because she can get pregnant and bear children for Jacob while Rachel cannot. This leads to Rachel giving her female servant to Jacob so the servant can get pregnant by Jacob and Rachel can claim the child as her own.

This plan works for a while, and the sisters are on an equal footing, but everything changes when Leah also gives her female servant to Jacob to become pregnant so Leah can claim the child as her own. The two sisters go back and forth like this for years, with Leah, Leah's servant, and Rachel's servant all giving birth to Jacob's children. Eventually, many years later, Rachel conceives a child of her own, a boy named Joseph.

The Scriptures tell us that Jacob loves Joseph more than his other children. Due to a competitive, and some might say jealous, spirit that continues from the mothers down to the children, we learn that ten of Jacob's sons hate Joseph due to their father's favoritism toward him and eventually sell him into slavery, lying to their father that Joseph has been killed by a wild animal.

I want to pause at this point and consider the improbable idea that, in my opinion, the story of Jacob, his two wives, the concubines, and all their children is a story about love: Rachel loves Jacob; Leah loves Jacob; Jacob loves his wives (although he loves one wife more than the other); Leah loves her children; Rachel loves her children; the children love their father; and Jacob loves his children (but he loves one child more than the others).

Although I think the story is about love, I did not say that the love displayed is healthy. I am also not saying that the characters in this arc of the Genesis story do not truly love each other. Rather, their love for each other is clearly tainted. One of the unique things about Jacob and his family is that the sisters each love Jacob so much and want nothing more than to have their love for him returned that they are willing to compete against each other. Likewise, Jacob's sons each love him so much that they are willing to gang up and kill Joseph, whom they believe is keeping them from experiencing the fullness of their father's love.

Unfortunately, what we read in Genesis about Jacob, his wives, and their children is not uncommon. The narrative is part of the ancestry stories that form the foundation of Israelite culture, and conflict and jealousy are part of these early stories.

The female servants of Rachel and Leah are not the first women to be handed off to another woman's husband so that a child could be conceived. Indeed, Abraham's wife Sarah, after learning that God would allow her to give birth to a child in her old age, becomes impatient with God's timetable and gives her female servant Hagar to Abraham so she could get pregnant by him and give birth to a child that Sarah could claim as her own. (Does this sound familiar?)

As in Jacob's story, jealousy takes center stage. Sarah is jealous of Hagar, and Hagar thinks she is better than Sarah due to her pregnancy. Eventually, Sarah mistreats Hagar, who then flees. Although Hagar returns to the family, the relationship between the two women is permanently strained. Similarly, Ishmael, the child Hagar births, grows to become a man with twelve sons of his own. (Does this also sound familiar?) Ishmael experiences similar tension with his family, so much so that God declares to Abraham that Ishmael would always be in conflict with his brothers.

Within the story of God's children, it seems that every generation has produced an individual who has been in conflict with another individual, leading to major consequences for God's children. However, by the end of each generation—or the end of that individual's story—God has found a way to turn the conflict into a blessing. In the story of Joseph, God takes unhealthy love and jealousy and blesses the nation of Egypt so that it can grow and prosper in ways unimaginable. And when the people of that nation think they are about to starve, God uses a man who has been sold into slavery by his brothers years before to save them from death, to restore their broken relationships, and to bring their story full circle.

I think the story of Joseph is about several things: It is about unwise parenting and the consequences that follow when we do not treat all our children in a way that shows them that they are as valuable as their siblings. It is about the dreams for the future that God gives us and the knowledge that most people will not believe in our dreams as we do. It is about the lengths to which people will go when anger has taken root in their hearts. It is about the fact that we may experience negative consequences when we turn away from sin. It is about being willing to forgive people who do not reap what they sow. It is about never losing hope that God is involved in our lives, although we may grow impatient waiting for God to move on our behalf. And it is about receiving God's protection and provision when we experience dark times in life.

Although I know these things are the point of Joseph's story, what sticks with me most is that, throughout the history of God's intention to be in relationship with humankind, God has consistently used flawed people from families with flawed pasts and flawed relationships and flawed motives to change the world and shape it to how God would have it be. When I consider Joseph's story, what I think about first is that every character in the story is flawed: Jacob is not necessarily the best husband or father; Rachel and Leah are in competition with each other; the children compete for their father's attention; and even favored son Joseph comes across as spoiled at the beginning of the story.

Even so, God uses the situation to bring safety and provision to not only the members of Joseph's family, but also to the nation of Egypt. May we always remember that neither our flaws nor the flaws of our family will keep God from using us as part of God's larger story. Although we may focus on the individual stories we experience or witness, God uses them all to weave the narrative that we understand to be God's love for all humankind and creation.

LOVE IS MORE THAN A FEELING

The Sound of Music
Ruth 1:8-18

Based on *The Story of the Trapp Family Singers*, Maria von Trapp's memoir *The Sound of Music* is an award-winning musical and movie. The book describes the life of the von Trapp family whose patriarch, widowed naval commander Georg von Trapp, has been wooed by the Nazis to help them develop a stronger naval fleet, which he refuses to do on moral grounds. At their core, the book, musical, and movie are about love and the various ways in which it can be expressed.

The Sound of Music tells the story of how love keeps a family going after the loss of a wife and mother. It also tells the story of the love a father has for his children. Commander von Trapp's family of seven children is large by today's standards, and the commander's love for his children makes him want to improve their circumstances so they can once again feel the joy of having a mother. He is willing to marry a woman he does not love in order to bring his children a certain level of peace. However, the commander is not prepared to fall in love for real, and when he does, he has no idea what or whom is in store for him.

The lovely Maria is a young woman training to become a nun. She loves God severely and also loves the other nuns in her abbey. She wants nothing more than to serve God and humanity while still retaining her own personality. Maria is not prepared to accept love outside of God and the abbey, but love is on the way, nonetheless. As is the custom of the day when wealthy families often employ tutors to educate their children, it isn't long before Maria becomes the tutor for the von Trapp children. The relationship between Maria and the children starts out somewhat rocky—and the relationship between Maria and Commander von Trapp is even rockier—but love wins out in the end.

But the story is about more than just the love between a father and his children and the nun who becomes part of their family. It is also about the love that people have for their country when it is taking a turn for the worse. Commander von Trapp is dedicated to protecting his Austrian homeland, but after recognizing the growing influence and power of the Nazi party, he has a decision to make: Should he stay in the community he loves and fight to keep it free from Nazi influence, or should he walk away so he can protect the children he loves?

During all these interactions, love is more than just a feeling: it leads to decisions, some easy and some difficult. All the decisions, however, have long-term implications both for the decision maker and the ones whose fates are being decided.

The same is true of the people we are introduced to in the biblical story of Ruth, a short but important chapter in the overall narrative. It is out of love that God calls on a group of people to worship God alone, and it is through this calling that all of humankind will eventually be blessed. The theology—the understanding of the nature of God—to which we are introduced in the story of Ruth is subtle: God does not perform an outstanding miracle, nor does God subdue a fearful enemy or cause a miraculous event to occur. Instead, God shows the restorative power of love through normal, everyday relationships. Through the progression of sincere relationships between vulnerable people who face forces over which they have no control, God shapes the foundation for the future salvation of a people and of the world.

As we read the story of Ruth, we have a distinct advantage over the characters. As they experience what life throws at them in "real time," they fret and wonder if and how they will overcome their circumstances. Fortunately for them and us, we already know that they are going to be okay. We know that the discomfort they feel at the beginning of Ruth due to the deaths of the men in their lives will eventually be replaced with relief. The places where clouds of gloom and despair have previously hung low will eventually be replaced by the shining light of hope that follows God's intervention, even though at times it looks as though God is not in the picture. The uncertainty they face will ultimately be replaced with a clear affirmation of God's love.

We know that Ruth's story ends well because Ruth finds love again and remarries. A woman who is at first thought of as inconsequential is eventually revealed to have tremendous implications for, and impact on, history after she is identified as being in the lineage of Jesus. Imagine being Ruth, or her mother-in-law Naomi, or her sister-in-law Orpah and trying to understand the long road of pain they have begun to travel after the deaths of their husbands.

Ruth, Naomi, and Orpah face tremendous difficulties trying to live as widows in a society that does not recognize the value of women outside of their husbands. Husbands are the providers for the family; thus, without their husbands or another male figure in their lives, these three women are more likely to be cast aside than embraced. As the eldest of the three, Naomi understands the uphill battle she and her daughters-in-law face when she implores them to leave her and return to their families of origin. I do not think she tells them to leave because she does not love them; in fact, I imagine that she loves them greatly and wants the best for them.

Naomi wants her daughters-in-law to be able to lead a decent life, and she knows this is unlikely to happen if they stay with her and remain unmarried. I think what Naomi is trying to figure out on behalf of Ruth and Orpah is something honorable. She is trying to think through how they would experience healing and restoration amid tragedy.

Ruth's poetic response to Naomi's attempts to get her to leave and return to her birth family has been considered one of the clearest proclamations of love and faithfulness in the Bible and has been pointed to as a model for others to understand and follow. Ruth implies that the way for healing to occur is for the women to stay together, not go their separate ways. Their joint healing would not be facilitated by reconnecting with people who are no more than a distant memory.

Instead, healing for Ruth would occur through staying with the one with whom she has shared recent experiences and has built a bond of love. By taking this stand, Ruth models for us what it means to love someone so much that we are willing to put aside our own safety and well-being and become vulnerable, along with the loved one. Ruth's attitude and actions show us that when love for another is greater than our desire for personal safety, we can overcome the fear and doubt that seek to define and confine us.

As the story of Ruth begins, two women have lost their husbands, and one woman has lost her husband and two sons. To add insult to injury, a famine—the second in ten years—is making life even more difficult. In addition, the women live in a society that does not look kindly upon women without husbands.

I think there are similarities between the book of Ruth and our experiences in 2020 and 2021. While we may not know what it is like to live during the time of a famine, we all know what it is like to live with the uncertainty of not knowing what the future holds due to a global pandemic. I imagine that for much of 2020 and 2021, readers spent time trying to figure out how to keep their lives together and functioning. Although most of us likely did not lack adequate food, we are still able to acknowledge the fear inherent in not knowing what tomorrow will bring due to the volatility of both the economy and the job market.

Additionally, we can sympathize with the loss of a loved one, even when that loss is not due to a death: perhaps you lost a valued relationship to an illness or accident, or perhaps a long-term relationship ended abruptly over a political opinion or affiliation.

The truth that we find in the book of Ruth is that we do not have to experience life alone; we do not have to experience hard times in solitude; we do not have to face death, famine, or pandemics by ourselves. God designed us and blesses us to be in relationship with each other and to give strength to each other. God also wants us to be a faithful presence for each other. God brings healing and restoration to those in pain and to those struggling with our relationships with them. Conversely, God also brings healing and restoration to us when we are in pain through our relationships with others.

One of the most iconic scenes from *The Sound of Music* comes at the end of the performance when the family finally escapes harm at the hands of military officials by fleeing through the wilderness and scaling a mountain to reach freedom. This moment is made possible by love in action: Knowing that the Nazis are searching for the von Trapp family, the nuns at Maria's abbey hide the family, providing them protection and safe passage. The nuns are willing to risk their own safety to protect Maria and her new family. Through this sacrificial act, the family is saved and the nuns serve as God's hand of salvation.

I should point out the irony that in real life Maria von Trapp did not start out loving the commander. In fact, she wrote in her autobiography that although she did not despise him, she did not love him. While she cared for his children, she had no feelings for the man and was devastated when Commander von Trapp proposed to her—so much so that she ran away and returned to the abbey.

In tears, she talked to the other nuns about her despair in having to consider marrying him. One nun went so far as to tell her that getting married to von Trapp was a part of her sacrifice to God and was what God wanted her to do. With that in mind, Maria returned to von Trapp, head hanging down. But something strange happened after they were married. Maria said that over time she learned to love and cherish von Trapp more than she did the children. They even had three children of their own. She eventually said that the love she had for him grew to be the greatest love she had ever experienced in life.

In some ways love is as much a choice that leads to consistent action as it is an emotional feeling. Jesus exemplified this for us in his dying for us. It seems to me that Jesus' actions were driven by his intentional choice to love others and to be the one to restore relationships between God and humankind. That voluntary act was the pinnacle of love. May we each seek to imitate it in our own ways today.

THE VALUE OF AVOIDING EVIL INFLUENCES

The Producers
Psalm 1:1-6

Written by Mel Brooks and Thomas Meehan, *The Producers* is an adaptation of Brooks' 1967 directorial movie debut of the same name. In 1967, *The Producers* won an Oscar for best original screenplay, and the Broadway musical version won a Tony Award for every category in which is was nominated.

The story revolves around Max, a once-prosperous Broadway producer whose best days are a distant memory. Back in his day, Max had made a lot of money but had since fallen on hard times. Whereas he was once a man of means whose fame and power brought him into contact with A-list celebrities, he now lives hand-to-mouth, trying to romance wealthy, older women who he thinks can help finance his next theatrical production. At the beginning of the production, Max's financial books are being audited by a naïve, young accountant named Leo who has just discovered a $2,000 discrepancy related to Max's last play.

After discussing the missing money, Max convinces Leo to overlook the relatively minor fraud and not report it. While working through how to help Max get away with this financial irregularity, Leo has a revelation. He figures out that a producer could make more money by staging a musical that was a flop than by staging one that is successful because shares of the production could be oversold, and when the musical failed, no one would expect to recoup their money or want to audit the books of a failed production.

With that in mind, both men agree to produce what they believe will be the worst musical in history and keep the money that has been invested when the musical proves to be a failure.

The musical they push to produce is *Springtime for Hitler: A Gay Romp with Adolf and Eva at Berchtesgaden*. The horrendous title does not begin to describe the nature of the musical, which, as you can imagine, celebrates the life of Adolf Hitler. Both Max and Leo know the production will fail under a cloud of embarrassment after only one show, and they will take the money that has been invested and flee to Rio de Janeiro. Unfortunately, their plan backfires: *Springtime for Hitler* becomes a resounding overnight success due to the audience misinterpreting it, leaving both men with the challenge of trying to figure out how they will repay all the investors whom they were planning to dupe in the first place.

At its core, *The Producers* is about is the poor choices people are willing to make when they operate from a position of greed and are unhappy with what they already have or are not willing to live within their means. Max exemplifies this dissatisfied attitude, going so far as to sing, "Oh, Lord, I want that money!" *The Producers* is also about what can happen to us when we allow ourselves to be influenced by people who do not hold our same values. Leo starts out as a timid accountant who is afraid to do wrong, but after listening to Max and looking at what other people have, Leo gives into the temptation to follow Max's illegal scheme.

These two ideas—a dissatisfied attitude and overwhelming negative influences—are part of the theme of Psalm 1:1-6. Being satisfied with what God is doing in your life and understanding the value of not being influenced by unrighteous people is the message of the psalmist. Set within a poetic format, the psalms are a series of instructions for God's followers, but they are less a series of laws or rules and more a conversation between someone who wants to better understand their Creator and their Creator wanting to become known by that person.

The Psalms are Hebrew poetry, a type of poetry very different from the more familiar English and American poetry, particularly of the twentieth or twenty-first centuries. Hebrew poetry is less concerned with rhyming or following traditional structures; instead, it presents thoughts in a consistent

— THE VALUE OF AVOIDING EVIL INFLUENCES —

manner by repeating ideas and building upon itself. For example, Psalm 1 makes regular use of contrasts to get its point across: It contrasts the actions of righteous, God-fearing people against the unrighteous people who do not fear God.

This contrast is framed as the process of traveling along two divergent paths: one that leads to wisdom (living in ways that please God) and one that leads to destruction (living in ways that displease God). The writer emphasizes that the path of wisdom is a lonely one typically traveled in solitude while the path of destruction is filled with travelers. The lesson is that choosing the road of righteousness is not necessarily an easy or popular choice.

When you choose the road of righteousness, you have to be ready for peer pressure that may deter you from what God wants. In contrast, it may be easier to travel the road of unrighteousness because you will not be walking alone. The path of wisdom is a steady trek toward a better understanding of God and what pleases God through self-sacrifice and spiritual discipline. In contrast, the path of destruction is a self-centered slog that begins with walking with those who oppose God and becoming comfortable enough to first stand with them and then sit with them on a regular basis. Of this tendency for the unrighteous to go from walking to standing to sitting, Rolf Jacobson writes that, "Perhaps the idea is that sin is a temptation that one first tries out, later becomes accustomed to, and finally becomes a habit or lifestyle."[1] Following the path of unrighteousness is a steady trek toward becoming more comfortable with sin and less concerned with its consequences.

The psalmist wrote that the unrighteous—those people who are comfortable with sin—are unstable in life and are blown back and forth by the winds of circumstance. They have no foundation in this world; they are dissatisfied with life and have nothing in which to place their hope. In contrast, those people who follow the path of righteousness are blessed (happy and/or content) with what they have because they know it comes from God. People who seek to live righteously have a level of peace that the unrighteous do not have because such peace only comes from God.

Ultimately, it is the unrighteous road of greed and deception that eventually leads to Max, Leo, and the composer of *Springtime for Hitler* being imprisoned in the state penitentiary. You would hope that after experiencing the fruits of their unrighteous labors the three of them would turn over a new leaf and become righteous. Instead, while serving time Leo and the composer of *Springtime for Hitler* create a new musical called *Prisoners of Love* that is to be performed by their fellow inmates. Hard as it is to believe, this musical is even worse than the Hitler musical. Max continues his practice of selling shares of the musical—this time to other inmates and the prison warden. Max never seems to figure out that there is a better way to approach life or that his sins will always catch up to him.

Fortunately for readers of Psalm 1, the psalmist offers the pathway toward a better way of living—a way that can lead to satisfaction and peace. But, that way to peace is not necessarily easy. It will require something from each of us, as Jacobson states:

> The psalm offers the free and gracious gift of a better way. But to follow in this "way" that Psalm 1 recommends will require that we unlearn some bad habits. Chief among those bad habits is the habit of relying upon ourselves and seeking to be our own lords and masters. It will require that we relinquish our greedy grasp on what we think of as our own freedom and will. But when we do so, we will discover, as did the psalmist, that there is a better way, a way that is truly free.[2]

I pray that we all experience this type of freedom and peace as we seek to abide by the psalmist's words.

Notes

1 Rolf Jacobson, *The Book of Psalms* (Grand Rapids: Wm. B. Eerdmans Publishing, 2014), 61.
2 Ibid., 64.

CHOOSING WISDOM

The 25th Annual Putnam County Spelling Bee
Proverbs 1:1-7

The musical comedy *The 25th Annual Putnam County Spelling Bee* holds a special place in my heart. My wife, Melinda, and I had only been married for a few years when I tried to plan a romantic weekend getaway in Chicago for our anniversary. One dreary afternoon we boarded a train for Chicago and bid *adieu* to the snowstorm that was approaching St. Louis. Little did we know that the storm would follow us to Chicago. The following morning we woke to a foot of snow and frigid temperatures that I had never experienced before.

To make matters worse, the "fancy" hotel I had booked online was not as fancy in person. In fact, it was downright decrepit. When Melinda turned on the hair dryer and I tried to iron clothes at the same time, the power went out in the entire room. We ended up leaving the hotel and staying with a competitor.

One of the few things that did go well that weekend was watching *The 25th Annual Putnam County Spelling Bee* at a small theater company. When I bought the tickets, I had no idea what the musical was about—I was just trying to do something I thought Melinda would like. It turned out to be one of the funniest experiences we have ever had.

Written by composer and lyricist William Finn, and based on a book by Rachel Sheinkin, *The 25th Annual Putnam County Spelling Bee* musical was nominated for multiple Tony Awards during it Off-Broadway and Broadway runs. As the title suggests, the play is about a grade-school spelling bee, the bee participants, and the reasons that each is motivated to participate in the first place. Among the eight main characters and multiple secondary characters we meet one of the few adults present: Ms. Rona Lisa Peretti. She is the best realtor in Putnam County and a former spelling bee champion in her own right. She won the third annual spelling bee by correctly spelling the word *syzygy*, which means "yoked together" or "conjunction" (a word I doubt a grade-schooler would ever need to know).

As far as bee participants go, Olive Ostrovsky is the newest contestant, but she almost doesn't make it due to not having the $25 registration fee. When Ms. Peretti finds out that Olive doesn't have the fee, she takes pity on her because Olive reminds her of herself, and she lets Olive enter without paying. Throughout the bee, Olive keeps hoping that her father will make it to hear her spell correctly, but as usual her father is too busy with work. Not only is Olive's father perpetually absent due to work, but her mother is somewhere in India on a spiritual retreat. We learn that Olive's only consistent friend is her dictionary.

Then there is Leaf Coneybear. Leaf, who is homeschooled, had finished in third place in his school district's spelling bee and only made it to the Putnam County bee because the first- and second-place winners were attending the winner's bat mitzvah. Leaf is from a family of hippies who make their own clothing, and he and his siblings are all named after something in nature. Sadly, Leaf believes that he is not very bright. He is extremely nervous about participating in the spelling bee, so much so that when he is given a word to spell, he falls into a deep trance and his mind runs in multiple directions until he is brought back to the task at hand with only a few moments to spare.

Due to these trances, one of Leaf's consistent struggles is living up (or down) to other people's expectations of him, particularly those of his parents. Leaf struggles with concentrating, which causes him to make decisions that his parents believe are unwise—and they regularly let him know about their frustration with him. Leaf's heart is broken because his parents do not understand him.

Much like parents who are concerned about their children making wise choices, the authors of Proverbs provide readers with a roadmap for how to consistently make decisions that will help life go well. Proverbs belongs to the "wisdom literature" genre, the purpose of which is to guide readers through the process of character formation. By discussing how personal character can be shaped and how a godly character can have an impact on a person or community, the writers of Proverbs help readers understand what it will take for them to please God.

Such character formation would not be forced upon a person by God, nor would God do something miraculous to cause a person to understand how their character should look. Instead, a person who wants to understand what God is looking for from them will need to learn from the experiences of others who have already committed themselves to trying to live in ways that please God. Dr. Kathryn Schifferdecker writes, "Wisdom literature seeks to teach its readers/hearers ... the attitude and means by which to live well. This kind of common-sense wisdom is based not on revelation (no burning bushes here) but on experience and observation. Nevertheless, it is grounded in a right relationship with God."[1]

According to Solomon, the primary author of Proverbs, the first step to understanding what a right relationship with God looks like—ostensibly the foundation of character formation—is to "fear" the Lord: "The fear of the Lord is the beginning of wisdom" (9:7 NIV). I know that the writer's use of the word "fear" here causes some people to be confused in their understanding of their relationship with God. In the twenty-first century, the word "fear" is not a happy word; in truth, it is a word that regularly divides people along political and social lines.

Thankfully, our relationship with God is neither political nor social: it is loving. In that sense, we do not have to be afraid of God. The point of "fearing" the Lord is not to be in relationship with God from a position of being scared of the One who created us, but rather to be in relationship with God from a position of recognizing that we are the created and we have been invited to be in relationship with our Creator. What an awe-inspiring thing! Schifferdecker illuminates this idea when she writes, "At its most basic level, the fear of the Lord is the knowledge that God is God, and we are not."[2]

As we recognize God as the "Great I Am" (and ourselves as not), we should be in awe that God seeks to have an intimate relationship with us aand therefore should approach God reverently, to worship God in spirit and truth, to want to regularly communicate with God, and to live in a way that honors that relationship. When we see our relationship with God as an offer from God made to us from a position of unconditional love, and when we are aware of the differences between us being the created and God being the Creator, it becomes easier for us to have our characters shaped in ways that please God.

It also becomes easier to do the things that Solomon says are the evidence of wisdom and character formation in the remainder of Proverbs 1, for example: listening to our parents when we are young, not hanging around with people who might negatively influence us, not taking items that belong to other people, not intentionally harming other people, and being honest. The writer of Proverbs 1 tells us that by doing these things, we will be living in community in ways that please God and build habits that will allow us and others to not only exist, but also to thrive during challenging times. Most importantly, we will focus on the things God says are important instead of what the world considers important. Ultimately, the writer says that "fearing the Lord" and having a proper understanding of who God is are the first steps on the road to being truly wise and pleasing to God.

By the end of *The 25th Annual Putnam County Spelling Bee*, everyone's view of Leaf Coneybear has changed because he is one of the final three contestants—not bad for someone who considers himself not very smart. Unfortunately, Leaf is eliminated because he misspells the word *chinchilla*. (Interestingly, all the words Leaf is asked to spell during the bee are for North or South American rodents.) As an adult, Leaf's belief that he is smarter than how others perceive him is affirmed, and after he is diagnosed with ADD/ADHD, he finds out his childhood trances were a coping mechanism for his disability.

Like Leaf, I imagine that we all struggle under the expectations that others put upon us. The good thing is that we do not have to worry about what others think about us or our choices in life. Instead, we can embrace God's view of us and seek to follow the path that is laid out for us. The first step to following the path God has set out for us is to remember that God is God, and we are not, and that is okay.

Notes

1 Kathryn M. Schifferdecker, "Proverbs 1:1-7; 3:1-8 Commentary," https://www.biblia.work/sermons/proverbs-11-7-31-8-commentary-by-kathryn-m-schifferdecker/ (accessed April 17, 2021).

2 Ibid.

(IN THE END) YOU CAN WIN

The Wiz
Ecclesiastes 1:12-18

Frank Baum's classic tale, *The Wonderful Wizard of Oz*, is retold and updated in the musical *The Wiz: The Super Soul Musical "Wonderful Wizard of Oz."* Conceived and written in 1974 primarily by William F. Brown and Charlie Smalls, *The Wiz* has since been adapted into multiple formats. The characters, settings, and plot are essentially the same as the original book, except the cast of characters is entirely Black (*The Wiz* was one of the first successful Broadway musicals to sport an all-Black cast), and the musical score is influenced by African-American soul music.

In 1975, the Broadway production of *The Wiz* won seven Tony Awards, including Best Musical. Due to the success and buzz surrounding the musical, a big-budget film was produced in 1978 starring Diana Ross, Michael Jackson, Nipsey Russell, Mabel King, Lena Horne, and Richard Pryor.

In the movie version of *The Wiz*, the cornfields and rural landscapes are replaced by rundown cityscapes filled with derelict, graffiti-covered buildings, subway tracks that carry no passengers, and taxi cabs that are never in service. Munchkins are replaced with somersaulting Black youth performing the popular dances of the 1970s. It also includes a funkified, Motown-influenced soundtrack produced by Quincy Jones. My favorite song from the movie is "You Can't Win," sung by Michael Jackson who played the Scarecrow. After the movie came out, it was the favorite song of most of the kids in our Black school.

We are introduced to the Scarecrow on a typical morning. Every day he hangs in the cornfields outside derelict buildings in an urban landscape, contemplating philosophy and the meaning of life, and wishing that someone would help him get down off his pole so that he can begin to enjoy life. Instead of scaring crows away from the corn in the fields, the Scarecrow is taken advantage of by the crows, who know he cannot get down off his pole. Somehow the crows have convinced the Scarecrow that he is not very smart—but that they are—and that by not helping him get down, they are doing him a favor by protecting him from the dangers of the world. Whenever the Scarecrow questions the crows' intentions, they make him sing the crow anthem, "You can't win, you can't break even, and you can't get out of the game. / People keep saying things are going to change but they look just like they're staying the same"[1]

Throughout *The Wiz*, the Scarecrow regularly questions his own intelligence and doubts his ability to do anything good or experience anything worthwhile. He reminds us of a singing, straw-filled Eeyore from *Winnie the Pooh*. Have you ever felt like that before? That life is stacked against you and there is nothing good coming your way? I can admit that when I was a 20-something trying to figure out life, "You Can't Win" was my theme song.

To me, Scarecrow's song is a somewhat modern summarization of the book of Ecclesiastes from the scriptures of Israel. Ecclesiastes is part of the "wisdom literature" tradition of the Old Testament, and its title is essentially the pen name of the book's author. Church tradition identifies King Solomon, David's son who ascended to the unified throne of Israel and Judah after David's death, as the author of the book.

At the beginning of his reign, Solomon's claim to fame is his wisdom and his ability to make decisions that help both his people and his kingdom. By the end of his reign, however, Solomon's story has reversed direction. In 1 Kings 3, we learn that after Solomon ascends to the throne of his father, God visits him during a dream and asks Solomon what he wants as the new king. Instead of asking for riches or power, Solomon asks for wisdom to lead God's people in a way that would make God happy. In response to this prayer, God gives Solomon wisdom, riches, and power. Solomon uses that wisdom to make many good decisions on behalf of God's people.

Readers will likely remember one of Solomon's most famous first acts as king: Two women and two babies are brought before him. One of the babies is alive; the other has died during the night. Both women claim to be the mother of the living child, and neither claim the child that has passed. It is Solomon's job to figure out which woman is telling the truth. Solomon recommends cutting the baby in half and giving one piece to each mother. One mother agrees to this suggestion. The other, being the true mother and not wanting to see her child hurt, volunteers to let the other mother have the child just so the baby will stay safe. Solomon recognizes the woman's love for her child and returns the child to her.

Everyone in the land is amazed by Solomon's decision and praises his wisdom. His reputation for making wise decisions becomes known even outside the city of Jerusalem. The scriptures of Israel tell us that many other foreign leaders visit Solomon to gain insight into how he makes his decisions. His reputation is gold both throughout his land and in foreign countries.

Unfortunately, Solomon's ability to make wise decisions changes over time after he begins to marry women from foreign lands. At first, these marriages seem like wise decisions because they lead to pacts of peace with the lands the women come from. However, with peace comes the influence of other, competing gods. Solomon begins to incorporate foreign beliefs into his decision-making process, which leads him to no longer follow God as he should and to not make decisions that are blessed by God. Solomon struggles as a leader because he has lost favor with God. Throughout his reign, Solomon tries to document the many changes that are taking place in his life and in his thinking. Ecclesiastes is almost like a chapter of Solomon's diary where he openly discusses the results of his decisions.

In Ecclesiastes 1, Solomon writes: "Nothing makes sense! Everything is nonsense. I have seen it all—nothing makes sense! What is there to show for all of our hard work here on this earth? People come, and people go, but still the world never changes" (vv. 2-4 CEV). In other words, you can't win! Many readers will be more familiar with how the King James Version of the Bible conveys Solomon's words: "Vanity of vanities … all is vanity" (v. 2).

The Hebrew word for "vanity" is difficult to translate into English because it has multiple meanings. One of the most appropriate translations is "vapor" or "smoke," such as the kind that comes from a pipe or cigar. It signifies something that has no true substance and is usually foul, poisonous, and temporary. As quickly as it appears, it disappears.

In Ecclesiastes, it seems as though Solomon is saying that when you really think about it, life is like smoke—it has no real substance, form or understanding, and it really does not amount to much. You cannot hold onto it. You cannot shape it. You can only experience it for a few moments before it disappears. The writer acknowledges that he has tried to understand life by gaining as much wisdom as possible, which did not help him in the end. He has tried to understand life by experiencing all the pleasures he could imagine, which did not help him, either. Although he is able to experience more than most people would in many lifetimes, none of his experiences has brought him much pleasure.

I admit that even though the writer sounds quite depressed, the book of Ecclesiastes has some inspiring qualities, one of which is how the tone of the book changes over the course of its twelve chapters. It begins with a "woe is me because life has no meaning" quality, but by the end, the writer's attitude has transformed into, "do not worry about anything. God is in control. So, enjoy every day that God gives you as a gift."

The Scarecrow's story in *The Wiz* follows a similar trajectory to that of Ecclesiastes. His story begins with him singing the crow anthem, "You Can't Win." The Scarecrow's life reflects the futility of his trying to live according to the dictates of people who do not have his best interests at heart. But when he meets someone who truly cares for him (Dorothy), the Scarecrow's fortunes change. As he and Dorothy, the Tin Man, and the Cowardly Lion face challenges on their journey, the Scarecrow's confidence in himself grows.

When others are making unwise decisions, the Scarecrow is able to be the voice of reason and hope. In the end, the Scarecrow helps his friends experience victory over the obstacles they encounter. What begins as a sob story for the Scarecrow ends with him experiencing joy and recognizing the shining sun in his life.

I imagine that at some point in life everyone can empathize with both the writer of Ecclesiastes and with the Scarecrow. We have all at times felt as though life is futile because things are not turning out the way we want or need them to. At other times, I imagine that it seems as though someone or some group is trying to force us to remain in a position of powerlessness, stopping us from becoming all that we can be.

We learn from Ecclesiastes that life is a journey that has its ups and downs. And, yes, sometimes those downs last longer than we would like, but that does not mean we should lose hope. In the end, God is aware and active and intervenes. I think that if we had the opportunity to talk to Solomon, he would say that the point of life is not to always get our way and avoid discomfort; the point is to build a closer relationship with God because doing so pleases God. That is the definition of "winning."

Like Solomon and the Scarecrow, God is concerned about our outlook on life. Do we have a "woe is me" attitude, or do we welcome each new day with the attitude that God has given us life and we should make the most of it? After we acknowledge and face life's frustrations, we can acknowledge the One who helps us overcome those frustrations and embrace the peace that comes to us through the Holy Spirit.

Note

1 Charlie Smalls, "You Can't Win," *The Wiz:* original soundtrack. Universal City, CA: MCA/Motown, [1997] Universal City, CA: Universal Music & Video Distribution℗1997.

RECONCILED FOR GOOD

Wicked
Matthew 5:21-26, 38-42

The musical *Wicked: The Untold Stories of the Witches of Oz* is based on the 1995 novel *Wicked: The Life and Times of the Wicked Witch of the West* by Gregory Maguire. Like the other musicals, *Wicked* has enjoyed a long run on Broadway, has won multiple Tony Awards, and has been influential in theatrical culture. Like *The Wiz*, *Wicked* is a creative retelling of the back story that led up to Frank Baum's book, *The Wonderful Wizard of Oz*. If the *Wizard of Oz* was a children's fairytale, *Wicked* is anything but. Instead, it is a coming-of-age tale packed full of adult themes such as love, infidelity, racism, and classism.

A major facet of the musical is the political unrest causing upheaval in the land of Oz, unrest caused primarily by the social and political policies instituted by the Wizard of Oz, the de facto ruler. Most of the policies have negative effects on the inhabitants of Oz, who are considered to be outsiders or "impure," and which keep the different groups separated and at odds with each other. The racism and classism that grow from these policies are best understood through the relationship that forms between the story's two main characters: Galinda, who eventually becomes known as Glinda, the Good Witch; and Elphaba, who eventually becomes known as the Wicked Witch of the West.

Galinda is a social insider. She is physically beautiful and born into the aristocracy. She is also concerned about being upwardly mobile and climbing social ladders. But she is not very good at magic when the story begins. Elphaba, by contrast, is a social outsider born from an affair her mother had with a traveling salesman while her husband was out of town. Elphaba has green skin, sharp teeth, and a severe allergy to water.

Elphaba's father does not like her and instead dotes on her younger sister whose birth caused their mother's death. Elphaba acts much as she looks: monstrously. She is a loner and a social outcast but is inclined toward magic. Even her personal passions leave her on the outside: whereas most people do not care about animals, their well-being is important to Elphaba. She believes that the Wizard of Oz will help her show the world that the animals in the kingdom are worthy of being treated equally.

While in college, Galinda and Elphaba become roommates out of convenience, but a friendship quickly forms. Galinda learns magical skills from Elphaba while Elphaba learns how to be more acceptable in the eyes of society. Their relationship experiences ups and downs, mostly due to Galinda's attempts to embarrass Elphaba in the hopes of making herself look better. The two girls eventually meet the Wizard of Oz, during which time they learn that the Wizard is nothing more than an ordinary man with little magical power and a lot of selfish intentions.

At the conclusion of the meeting, the girls are left with a choice to make: Do they follow the Wizard and his ideas, which are causing pain and separation, or do they take a stand against him? Galinda chooses to follow the Wizard, but Elphaba chooses to follow her principles. Based on their choices, the two girls can no longer be friends, and they go their separate ways. What had once been a blossoming relationship is now torn apart with substantial repercussions for the two girls and the land.

In Matthew 5:21-26, Jesus addresses the subject of torn relationships. Matthew 5 is part of the Sermon on the Mount where Jesus is teaching his disciples what it means to be a member and representative of God's kingdom. Through his parables and teachings, Jesus tells listeners what God expects from their membership in God's kingdom, especially God's expectations for participating in human relationships.

As is his habit, Jesus challenges the crowd's understanding of the old teachings that influence their communities, such as the Tenth Commandment prohibition that it is a sin to murder another person (vv. 21-26). In the minds of Jesus' listeners, if they are at odds with someone but do not murder that person, then they are okay with God. They believe that if they do not commit acts of physical violence against their enemies, they are truly following God. Jesus pushes back against this idea as being too simple.

For Jesus, although committing acts of violence against others violates God's wishes for human relationships, the attitudes that people hold toward each other is as important as the actions they commit. Eric Barreto writes about Jesus' teachings on violence toward others, saying, "Jesus teaches, it is insufficient to avoid murdering someone; certain kinds of anger and insult can themselves be a form of violence to eschew."[1] While physical action against someone can lead to a person being held accountable in a court of law, holding the wrong attitude toward someone can lead to God passing judgment on the person holding the angry attitude.

Holding the right attitude toward other people is so important to God that Jesus tells his listeners a person should not make a sacrifice to God if they have not already sought to restore broken relationships with others. Jesus tells them that they should not even offer a sacrifice (the act of asking God for forgiveness for known and unknown sins) if they have not already asked for forgiveness from the person they have a broken relationship with. Instead of making a sacrifice to God, listeners are asked to first seek the forgiveness of those from whom they are estranged. In other words, reconciliation is the only way forward.

Reconciliation involves making a personal effort to improve a relationship. It requires acknowledging that something has gone wrong in the relationship and recognizing our part in the separation. It is not about waiting for someone else to be the bigger person or to apologize, nor is it enough to understand that something has gone wrong in a relationship. Jesus teaches his listeners that it is their responsibility—and ours—to start the process of mending what has been broken. Only after someone seeks reconciliation should they offer a sacrifice to their Creator. Jesus tells his listeners that God holds us individually responsible for maintaining and improving our relationships, fixing misunderstandings that may have occurred, and changing our perceptions of others. It is our responsibility to make things better.

One of the most impactful songs in *Wicked* is "For Good," sung by Elphaba and Galinda after they come face-to-face with each other years after their fateful meeting with the Wizard of Oz. After being separated for so long, they understand that this could be the last time they ever see each other. Instead of using it as an opportunity to rehash old grievances, they use it as an opportunity to reconcile, if even for a moment, when they sing, "It well may be that we will never meet again in this lifetime / So, let me say before we part so much of me / Is made of what I learned from you."[2]

If only our relationships could be healed through a Broadway musical! We all know that it takes much more than that; it takes self-sacrifice and—as the song says—admitting our part in misunderstandings.

I end this chapter with a question from Eric Barreto that is relevant to the subject of reconciliation. He asks: "[W]hat if broken relationships among neighbors, family, and friends are not just social obstacles among us but a barometer for our relationship to God too? What if the obverse of murder is not just avoiding killing but reparative reconciliation?"[3]

If it is true that our relationships with others reflect our relationship with God, then the next question should be: What does my relationship with God look like? Is the health of my relationship with God being reflected through the health of my other relationships? If it is, good! If it is not, right now is the perfect time to initiate reconciliation in those relationships that need it.

Notes

1 Eric Barreto, "Commentary on Matthew 5:21-37," https://www.workingpreacher.org/commentaries/revised-common-lectionary/sixth-sunday-after-epiphany/commentary-on-matthew-521-37-4 (accessed March 21, 2021).

2 Stephen Schwartz, "For Good," *WICKED: a New Musical: Original Broadway Cast Recording*. New York: Decca Broadway, 2003.

3 Barreto, "Commentary."

YOU DON'T HAVE TO WORRY

The Lion King
Matthew 6:25-34

Originating as a Disney cartoon in 1994, *The Lion King* musical (after an interrupted schedule due to Covid-19) is still running on Broadway after more than 9,000 performances, making it Broadway's third-longest-running show in history. The theatrical release is Disney's third-highest grossing cartoon, and the show has made more than $1 billion on Broadway alone, making it the highest-grossing Broadway production of all time. Between the movie and the musical, *The Lion King* has won numerous awards including Oscars, Golden Globes, and Tony Awards.

The movie and musical explore the life of a lion cub named Simba and his transition from an innocently mischievous child to the king of his pride. When the story begins, Simba struggles with understanding what it means to be the future king of his land. Mufasa, the reigning lion king and Simba's father, does his best to help the young cub understand their collective responsibility to think first about others and not themselves.

Because of his heavy duties as king, Mufasa is often worried: He worries about Simba, the lion pride, and the other animals in the kingdom. Although Simba is a child, he too worries about what it would mean for him to one day become king and how he would take care of others. The one character in the story who clearly does not think about others, however, is Scar, Mufasa's evil brother. Scar resents his brother and resents the fact that his young nephew Simba is next in line as the leader of the Pride Lands. Unfortunately, Mufasa and Simba are unaware that Scar is plotting to kill Mufasa and blame Simba.

Does any of this sound familiar? Are you reminded of any of the stories in the Bible? The plot of *The Lion King* makes me think about some of the events that occur later in the life of King David, in particular when one of his sons plots to usurp the throne. This son resents his father and brothers and schemes to gain the support of the people over David and kill his brothers so there will be no competition for David's throne.

In *The Lion King*, Scar murders Mufasa and convinces Simba that it is his fault that his father has died. Much like Moses after he murdered an Egyptian, Simba flees the land in fear and shame, and finds himself on the backside of the desert. Simba eventually befriends a meerkat named Timon and a warthog named Pumbaa who sing the now-famous song, "Hakuna Matata." *Hakuna Matata* is a Swahili phrase meaning "no troubles" or "no worries."

In Swahili culture, the phrase is used to help alleviate a person's concerns and encourage that person to move on with life instead of remaining paralyzed. Timon and Pumbaa use the phrase slightly differently in *The Lion King* as an encouragement to not be overwhelmed by challenges that we cannot control. The phrase seeks to encourage people to acknowledge life's challenges while still finding a way to move forward.

How to face life's challenges is at the heart of Matthew 6:25-34 when Jesus tells his listeners to not worry about what life throws at them but instead to trust that God will continue to care for and provide for them. In Matthew 6, the words of Jesus are part of his teachings that occurred during the early days of his ministry in Galilee. Chronologically, these teachings are part of the Sermon on the Mount.

The overarching theme of the Sermon on the Mount, which is the largest collection of Jesus' teachings, is about trusting God and giving oneself to God in a sacrificial manner as an act of worship. The Sermon on the Mount begins with the Beatitudes: Blessed are the peacemakers; blessed are the humble; blessed are those who mourn. Jesus uses the Beatitudes to describe the character of those who are members of God's kingdom—a character they can only develop with God's help.

Another of Jesus' major teachings is the "Lord's Prayer," which I think Jesus shared as a way of pushing back against the practice of performing a good deed for personal recognition instead of doing good for the sake of doing good. The habit of the day was to make a spectacle of oneself when praying or giving a gift to show everyone how holy you were. Through the "Lord's Prayer," Jesus tells his followers to stop worrying about what other people think and instead to perform good deeds only for God's approval.

Another reason that Jesus teaches his listeners the "Lord's Prayer" is to remind them that God is the One who provides for their daily needs. He indicates as much in Matthew 6:11 when he says, "Give us this day our daily bread."

In Matthew 6:25-34, Jesus speaks to his listeners again about trusting that God will provide and not worrying about what they will eat, drink, or wear. Those listeners who consider themselves to be members of God's Kingdom will need to learn to make God, God's power, and God's faithfulness their focus.

In Matthew 6:19-24, Jesus tells his followers that their hope for life cannot be found in the things they accumulate through money or work as these things are temporary and will eventually fade away. Physical items cannot be taken with us in death, and our accumulated worldly possessions will eventually fight for attention with God—the One who provided them in the first place. Being distracted by material things is in direct opposition to making God our primary focus.

Throughout his ministry, Jesus emphasizes the idea that possessions are given by God and not to be held onto tightly. Instead, they are to be shared to improve the lives of others. Jesus wants his listeners to remember that the gifts they receive from God are not just for them, and when his listeners share their gifts with others, God can replace what has been given away. Stanley Hauerwas follows up on this idea when he writes:

> Abundance, not scarcity, is the mark of God's care for creation. But our desire to live without fear cannot help but create a world of fear constituted by the assumption that there is never enough. Such a world cannot help but be a world of injustice and violence because it is assumed that under conditions of scarcity our only chance for survival is to have more.[1]

This statement reflects the teachings of Jesus—Jesus wants his followers to trust in him more than they trust in their possessions. He even goes so far as to say that having possessions can make it difficult for people to enter God's kingdom because people have a tendency to desire their possessions more than they desire residency in the Kingdom. Through the Sermon on the Mount, the "Lord's Prayer," and other teachings, Jesus challenges his listeners to trust more in him and God than in worldly possessions.

Jesus wants his listeners to understand that he alone is the embodiment and fulfillment of God's eternal promise to supply the needs of humankind. I also think that Jesus wants his listeners to develop the mindset that since he is the embodiment of our daily bread (which comes from God), we do not have to hold onto worldly things. Instead, we should recognize that through the abundance of God's gracious love, God will take care of us regardless of whether we think we have too much or too little. Worrying about our life and circumstances does not have to be our focus.

As with most Disney musicals, in the end everything turns out okay for Simba, the young lion king. "Hakuna Matata" becomes Simba's song, and he develops meaningful relationships with both Timon and Pumbaa. Not worrying is good for Simba in one way—he is able to put the pain of the past behind him and build a meaningful life for himself. However, in another way, not worrying makes Simba forget his responsibilities as the leader of his pride and the land, which allows his uncle Scar to take over and bring the community to the brink of ruin. After the unforeseen appearance of a childhood friend, Simba returns to the Pride Lands and eventually takes his rightful place as king.

In our own lives, things will turn out well because Jesus is our daily bread and God is our Creator who watches over us and cares for us. That does not mean our lives will be worry-free, but we can rest assured that no matter what we face in life, God, through his Son, Jesus, will care for and provide for us in the here and now and will give us eternal security in the afterlife.

This promise of security should encourage us to live out the Beatitudes and embody the teachings of Jesus. Hauerwas summarizes this idea well when he writes:

[T]hose who would follow Jesus are taught that we have time to care for one another through small acts of mercy because God's mercy is without limit. Abundance, not scarcity, is the mark of God's kingdom. But that abundance must be made manifest through the lives of a people who have discovered that they can trust God and one another. Such trust is not an irrational gesture against the chaos of life, but rather a witness to the very character of God's care of creation.[2]

Notes
1 Stanley Hauerwas, *Matthew* (Ada, MI: Brazos Press, 2015), 82.
2 Ibid.

LOVE, REGARDLESS

Rent
Luke 8:26-39

The musical *Rent* was conceived for the stage by writer Billy Aronson and composer Jonathan Larson and is a retelling of Puccini's classic Parisian opera *La Bohème*. Both *La Bohème* and *Rent* explore the bohemian lifestyles of a community of artists, musicians, singers, and their friends and the struggles they experience in life and love while trying to make it big in their respective cities. *La Bohème* is a staple in the opera world, and *Rent* was a huge Broadway success, winning multiple awards, including a Pulitzer Prize for Drama and a Tony Award for Best Musical. After its twelve-year run on Broadway, *Rent* was made into a movie musical in 2005.

The titles of *La Bohème* and *Rent* are strategic and serve as reference points for what the characters in each story will experience. *La Bohème* refers to the word "bohemian," which is a nontraditional way of living sometimes followed by artistic people in which they willingly accept certain levels of poverty. The word "rent" has multiple meanings, but usually refers to the money paid to a landlord to live in a residence. Throughout *Rent*, most of the characters struggle to afford the high cost of living in their city.

Rent, however, can also mean to tear something apart. In the musical *Rent*, a number of characters experience events that threaten to tear them and their cherished relationships apart. When I think about *La Bohème* and *Rent*, I cannot help but think that this is the primary theme of both musicals. The question in both stories is: How can the the characters overcome their challenges without allowing their lives to be torn apart?

Although *La Bohème* takes place in the beautiful city of Paris, it is set in a less well-to-do neighborhood where the residents struggle to make ends meet. The characters are poor, many of them barely scraping by. They have few resources or opportunities. Their poverty is reflected in the dirty streets, dank buildings, and cold, dimly lit apartments of the background scenery. Some people might say that the personal lives of the characters in the opera are just as dirty.

Rent takes places in New York's Alphabet City, a set of intersections located in Lower Manhattan's East Village where artistic creativity is housed and regularly on display. *Rent* also showcases the shadow of sexual promiscuity and the AIDS epidemic that results from such poverty, and most of the characters could be considered "unclean." When I use the term, "unclean," I mean that most of the characters would likely not be considered worthy of having relationships with good, God-fearing people.

Luke 8:26-39 explores Jesus' interaction with an unclean man from a town so unclean that neither the man nor the town merit a showing of God's grace. Yet, Jesus has a powerful interaction with this man that shows the power of Jesus to heal sickness, disease, and sin.

Beginning in Luke 5, the author shares a series of stories that highlight Jesus' ability to heal people both physically and spiritually. In chapter 5, after calling his first disciples, Jesus heals a leper and a paralyzed man. In chapter 6, he heals a man with a withered hand then preaches his famous "Beatitudes" sermon. In chapter 7, Jesus proclaims healing on a Roman soldier's servant—without even seeing the servant—raises to life a widow's dead child, and proclaims forgiveness upon a woman whose reputation is poor. With each of these interactions, Jesus proclaims and fulfills God's mandate to love unclean people while also showing his authority to proclaim people changed for the better despite what others think of them.

In Luke 8, Jesus and his disciples sail across the Sea of Galilee and prepare to enter the town of Gerasenes, a Gentile city under Roman control that had been established by Alexander the Great. Gerasenes is likely not a town friendly to Jesus or to the beliefs of Jewish people. It is considered an unclean place that Jesus and his disciples should avoid or enter only if it mandatory. The author of Luke emphasizes the uncleanliness of the town by highlighting the fact that a herd of pigs—ceremonially unclean animals—is grazing openly.

As Jesus and his disciples exit their boat, they are met by a man who oozes uncleanliness from every pore: He is likely a Gentile; he is naked; he is homeless and lives in a graveyard; he is dirty and violent; and he is either demon-possessed or suffering from a mental disability that causes him to act in a menacing way.

How often have you interacted with people like this man? In St. Louis, Missouri, the city I call home, you are likely to run across someone like this every day. During the five years I was a police officer, I used to regularly interact with people like this in what were considered some of the most unclean neighborhoods in the city. People fitting this description can be found walking the streets every day somewhere in the city of St. Louis; they sit outside restaurants, gas stations, and grocery stores talking to themselves and yelling at people who are not there. They ask for change, food, and anything else that their minds can come up with. They also scare many people who encounter them.

If you have ever encountered a person such as the demon-possessed man in scripture, how did you respond? I ask this not to be judgmental, as I understand that an encounter with a person who may be struggling with mental health challenges or drug addiction can be unsettling. Our natural instinct is to go in the opposite direction to keep ourselves and our loved ones safe.

Instead of going in the opposite direction, according to Jewish protocol, Jesus talks with this man. Jesus learns that the man's affliction is called "legion" because the man is controlled by not one but many afflictions. Just as the titles *La Bohème* and *Rent* hold significant meaning, so too does the word "legion" hold a significant meaning for Luke's readers. In the Roman army, a legion was upwards of six thousand military personnel in formation ready to fight. Eventually, legion began to be used as a symbolic term that signified an infinitely large number of opponents.

Luke could not use this word without his readers knowing these two meanings. Luke's readers would have keyed in on the fact that the man was suffering from multiple afflictions that made him an outcast to both his family and his city. They would have also known that the town Jesus was about to enter and the person he was about to interact with were living under the control of a foreign power that stood in opposition to the one true God that they and Jesus worshiped.

Instead of going in the opposite direction when the man approaches him, Jesus leans in and helps the man by casting the demons out of him and into the herd of pigs that has been grazing nearby. Jesus sends the unclean spirits into the unclean animals, who then rush down an embankment into the lake to their death. Free from the afflictions that have severely impacted his life, the man is now clean. He is no longer suffering from his mental health challenges, nor is he naked, violent, and screaming at people. He is a new man.

Word immediately spreads throughout the town about what Jesus has done for this man. But instead of people celebrating, they are afraid—not of the man, but of Jesus. It seems as if the kind act Jesus performed is being held against him. Instead of inviting Jesus to help others suffering from demon possession or mental health afflictions, the townspeople beg him to leave. (Why do they do this? Truthfully, I do not know. If this had happened to someone I know, I would have celebrated the change and asked Jesus to help me with whatever was wrong with my life.)

I wish I had some dazzling theological statement to offer, but instead, I am left thinking back over my life and wondering if I have ever responded in such a way when God has done something miraculous for another person. I ask myself if I have ever been afraid of how God has blessed someone else. It seems as though Jesus recognizes the tension in the community and instead of fighting against it, he accepts the fear of the locals and decides to leave and continue his ministry of healing and blessing elsewhere.

Before he leaves, however, the man he has healed begs Jesus to go with him. Jesus responds by telling the man to stay in his hometown and reveal to everyone the miracle that has been performed in his life. (I admit that this is one of the weirder resolutions to a situation that Jesus has been involved in. There is no neat and tidy way to tie this passage together.)

I understand that while we can try to mimic Jesus' interactions with the demon-possessed man by recognizing that what we see in people is not always what is truly going on with them, we may not truly know or understand what they are struggling with. We may see people who live strange lives that do not fit our preconceived ideas of what a good life should be; they may actually be carrying the weight of mental illness or simply living a life that is out of their control. Such things may cause them to act in ways that are foreign to what we understand or have experienced ourselves.

People such as this do not need for others to treat them as though they are unclean and unworthy of being in a relationship. They need most for others not to run *away* from them or to lecture them; instead, they would benefit from others running *toward* them and being willing to help them. This is the first step in having people see and understand that God cares for them.

God's love lived out by each of us will be measured in ways that we sometimes overlook. God will measure our love for others by means that may seem insignificant to us but will get to the heart of how God loves. This means walking with people through strange times, sharing cups of coffee and helping them work through a life challenge, helping someone repair a bridge that was once burned, or simply being a shoulder for someone to cry on. This is how we can live out the Beatitudes that Jesus preached about before he went on his healing tour. May we be blessed to bring healing to other people's lives.

WE DON'T HAVE TO BE WORLDS APART

Big River
Acts 10:34-35

The musical, *Big River: The Adventures of Huckleberry Finn*, is based on the 1884 book, *The Adventures of Huckleberry Finn*, by Mark Twain. The book and musical tell the story of a teenage Huckleberry Finn, his friend Tom Sawyer, and a runaway slave named Jim who embark on adventures along the Mississippi River during the late nineteenth century. Both the book and the musical explore the impact of unfulfilled dreams.

As the musical opens, Huck has been adopted by two older women who are set on civilizing him and saving his soul. Instead of being civilized and saved, however, Huck dreams of adventure and love. Jim the slave struggles with civilization and salvation of a different kind. He dreams of being treated in a civilized manner by people who do not see him as fully human. He dreams of equality and opportunity. Although Huck and Jim live in different worlds, both characters hold onto a common hope, which is to be free.

Both Huck and Jim yearn to be free of others' expectations of them and free of the physical confines they both face. Both struggle with the idea of freedom, and they face pressing questions, some of which come from within themselves: Is life fair? Did God create all people to be equal? If so, why are some people not treated that way?

Huck, a boy of adventure, also has to deal with the question of whether he is willing to be made into a civilized young man by the women who care for him. Jim has to deal with the question of whether he would allow himself to continue being treated as an "other." Would he allow himself to be sold to yet another master who would not treat him well? Neither Huck nor Jim wait for someone else to answers their questions. Instead, they both escape their circumstances and float down the Mississippi River toward freedom, both physical and psychological.

A theme common to both *Huckleberry Finn* and *Big River* is the need to ask and answer questions, both personal and corporate. The most interesting question of the story to me is this: Do we have to accept the future that someone else has planned for us? In a sense, Acts 10 deals with this by asking a series of important questions such as the following:

- Are we required to follow older traditions of how we view relationships?
- Are we locked into interacting with people or with God based on other people's expectations?
- Are we allowed to imagine new ways of thinking about what it means to live in relationship with God and with each other?

In Acts 10 we are introduced to Cornelius, a Gentile official who works for the Roman army. He is not necessarily a bad man, and at first glance he seems to be a very good man. He is a "God-fearer," as are the people in his household. He worships at the local synagogue, acknowledging the God of Israel as the one true God and following some of the Jewish customs such as making sacrifices and offerings, giving gifts to the poor, and supporting building projects that benefit Jews in the area. Although Cornelius is a good man who does good things, he likely is not good enough in the sight of many Jews in the community because he is not Jewish. Jewish tradition would classify him as "other."

Cornelius is visited by an angel of God who tells him that God has recognized his heart and personal sacrifice. His prayers to God and his gifts on behalf of other people have not been ignored. God has recognized and appreciated Cornelius' actions. He is pleasing to God. The angel of the Lord directs him to find a man named Simon Peter who is staying in the nearby town of Joppa. The angel does not tell Cornelius why he has to do this, but Cornelius complies with the angel's wishes.

The following day, Simon Peter, one of Jesus' disciples, is sitting on a roof trying to figure out what he wants for lunch. As he dreams about his next meal, he experiences a vision in which a huge sheet descends from heaven. The sheet contains all kinds of animals, including those that Jews believe are unclean and not fit to eat. As Peter watches the sheet descend from heaven, a voice commands him to eat the animals on it. This is unacceptable for Peter, a devout Jew.

Throughout his life, Peter has been taught to read the right books, visit the right places, avoid the wrong people, and eat the correct food. Thus, Peter refuses to do as the voice commands. His refusal is met with the statement, "What God has made clean, you must not call profane" (v. 15). As you can imagine, Peter is stunned by this response. Why would God ask him to eat unclean animals? Before he can come up with an answer, the Spirit of God tells him that "unclean people" (Gentiles) would come looking for him and that he should go with them. Shortly thereafter, Cornelius' men arrive looking for Peter to take him to their leader, and Peter willingly goes with them.

This is a significant development in the lives of both a devout Jew named Peter and a Gentile named Cornelius and should not be glossed over. Jews did not fraternize with Gentiles, and vice versa. Cornelius represents Rome's military power—the power that exerts control over Peter's people. For Peter, spending time with a Gentile such as Cornelius is akin to eating unclean meat that has come down on a sheet from heaven. Yet, God compels Peter to take the first step to do just that.

Upon meeting Cornelius, Peter shares with everyone the message of God's redeeming love found in Jesus, and something strange and unexpected happens. The Holy Spirit falls upon all who hear Peter's words, and they speak in tongues. These "other" people experience the same thing that Peter and the disciples who follow Jesus experience. This is not something that could be faked or made up; it has come directly from God.

People who were once considered unclean and unacceptable are now shown to be as "clean" and acceptable as Peter. People who were once considered to be "other" are now part of the same spiritual family. Those who Peter once called outsiders are now called children of God because God has said they are acceptable. It is Peter's duty to get in line with God's thinking.

Gentiles are now a part of God's family. They can officially be converted, transferred into, welcomed into, and included in God's family in and through Christ. That is a powerful thing for Peter to see. These outsiders exhibit the same qualities that he and the other disciples exhibit. People who, at the beginning of the day, were worlds apart, are now spiritual brothers and sisters.

Similarly, people such as the slave Jim and Huck Finn, who see the same stars through different eyes and who experience life from different vantage points, also now see life through a similar lens. Those people who had previously been worlds apart are now going to experience salvation through the same Holy Spirit. This is because of the truth of the gospel of God's love—the truth that Jesus died to reconcile all people to their common Creator. This is the heart of the gospel message that Peter preaches. Jim and Huck and Peter and Cornelius are not the only ones who must deal with this issue of differing worlds or clean versus unclean. We all must.

Although we do not usually use words such as clean and unclean to describe people, we do use words such as liberal and conservative, Republican and Democrat, rich and poor, the haves and have-nots. When we use these terms, we are describing people who we think are "in" or "out." We are determining whether such people deserve or do not deserve our respect, mercy, and love. We use these words to describe who we think is worthy of God's respect, mercy, or love. Ultimately, we use these words to describe who we think should be a part of God's family and who should not.

In acting this way, we fail to remember that, like Peter, God has called us to reach out to those whom we think are unclean or unworthy of our time and compassion. We forget that God's Spirit sends us to people who need to know that God loves them just as they are and wants to be in relationship with them. God's love overcomes uncleanliness and otherness. My prayer for us, as our nation works through all that keeps us separated, is that we embrace Peter's lead and welcome the opportunities that God brings our way to form new relationships with people we would not necessarily expect to be friends with.

BE CAREFUL WHAT YOU FEED

Little Shop of Horrors
Romans 12:9-21

The musical comedy *Little Shop of Horrors* tells the story of a boy and his adorable, bloodsucking, seven-foot-tall Venus Flytrap plant. *Little Shop of Horrors* originated as a low budget, black-and-white film in 1960 written by Charles B. Griffith and directed by Roger Corman. The movie, which cost $30,000 to make, received decent reviews when it was released as a "B" movie reel (the second half of a two-feature film show where the "B" reel was expected to be less popular and make less money than the primary film). The movie's popularity and influence, however, eventually grew through word-of-mouth support and multiple showings on television. *Little Shop of Horrors* eventually reached cult status.

In 1982, the black-and-white movie was reimagined as a comedic rock musical. Its beginnings were small, premiering in an Off-Off-Broadway theater. As the show grew in popularity, it was staged in a larger Off-Broadway theater for more than five years and eventually became popular enough to open on Broadway. As a result of the musical's popularity, Frank Oz, better known as a puppeteer and the voice of the fictional characters Miss Piggy and Yoda, directed a $25-million movie based on the musical in 1986. This version of the story was well received and was nominated for multiple Academy and Golden Globe Awards.

Although *Little Shop of Horrors* is told in three distinct platforms, they all follow the same basic plot. A young man named Seymour works in a plant store and lives a simple life, but he is unfulfilled because he is in love with a woman named Audrey with whom he will never have a relationship.

Unfortunately for Seymour, Audrey is already in a relationship with a man who does not deserve her. Seymour does eventually build a relationship with someone—just not the person he was anticipating.

Through a series of strange events, Seymour comes to possess a plant that he names Audrey Jr. in the 1960 movie and Audrey II in the 1982 musical and 1986 movie. In all three versions of the story, Audrey the plant is anything but ordinary. Audrey II can talk, reason, sing, and tell Seymour what it wants. And what it wants most of all is … blood. Blood sustains Audrey II and allows the plant to grow. Thus, Seymour faces the challenge of securing enough blood to feed Audrey II.

At first, Seymour feeds the plant with his own blood. But as it grows and its appetite increases, the plant demands more and more blood, making a regular refrain to Seymour, "Feed me!" Seymour is led to believe that if he feeds the plant, all of his dreams will come true. The plant eventually convinces Seymour to kill those people whom Seymour thinks do not really deserve to live. And who is one of the first people Seymour identifies as not really deserving to live? Why, the boyfriend of the woman of his dreams, of course.

Over time, Seymour comes under the influence of the plant in ways he could never anticipate. Seymour starts out as a loving and kind young man, but over time, he begins to care less about others and more about the things he wants. At first, killing causes Seymour to experience grief, but the more he does it, the easier it becomes. Seymour has fallen into the clutches of the plant physically, emotionally, and spiritually.

You may be wondering what *Little Shop of Horrors* has to do with Romans 12. In my opinion, there are aspects of the story told in the *Little Shop of Horrors* that are present in the lives of the people Paul writes to in his letter to the Romans. The scholarly consensus is that Paul did not plant the church at Rome. Rather, it is believed that someone who had been present on the Day of Pentecost in Acts 2 traveled to Rome and shared their faith with the people there, and from that testimony sprang a small community of Jesus followers.

What started out as a gathering of a handful of people eventually grew into a larger, regular meeting that included both Jewish and Gentile households. Paul had heard many positive things about this group of believers and looked forward to eventually fellowshipping with them in person. But until that day comes, he has to be content with beginning a conversation with them through his letter that covers several topics he feels are important for the church at Rome to understand.

One of those topics is the idea that after a person begins to understand that God wants to be in relationship with humans and the rest of creation, and that Jesus embodied this desire through his sacrificial act on a cross and his ascension to heaven, a person who believes that truth should exhibit new qualities in relation to how they live.

In Romans 12, Paul tells his readers that God wants God's children to be different from the world by grounding their lives in love for others above love for self. Paul is trying to get his readers to understand that God-pleasing transformation includes the idea of love becoming the structuring reality of their lives. Membership in God's family through Jesus should lead a person to change on multiple levels. Spiritual change is important, but change related to how a person views and treats others also is important.

In Romans 12, Paul expresses this idea through a list of imperatives that are grounded in the idea of love. In essence, Paul encourages his readers to embrace the idea of loving others through sacrificial actions such as these:

- doing what is right for others
- finding joy in helping others
- acting with kindness
- not seeking revenge against enemies
- being compassionate to everyone including one's enemies
- seeking peace with everyone including one's enemies
- being intentional about defeating evil through godly actions

Paul teaches us that since God loves people and shows this love through the sacrifice of Jesus on the cross, members of God's family should show a similar kind of love to others, whether or not these others are a part of God's family. In the early chapters of his letter to the Romans, Paul reviews the history of humankind and how all people, regardless of ethnicity or other criteria, have willingly participated in the process of being separated from God.

Instead of seeking God and turning to their Creator, humankind has turned away and followed their own desires. A force is always calling to humans, trying to draw their attention away from the One who wants what is best for them. Paul identifies this force as sin, writing that when sin calls a person's attention away from God, it is not because sin wants the best for a person. Instead, when attention is drawn away from God, sin is fed, growing stronger, and becoming more capable of dominating a person's life.

In Romans 12, Paul is not simply asking his audience to practice self-control. He is challenging them to imitate God's love by initiating good things in other people's lives, whether those other people are cherished family members or current enemies. Paul knows that throughout their journey as Christians, the members of the church at Rome would hear sin's call to feed it by acting in a self-centered way, being vindictive, holding grudges, or letting evil have the last word. Instead of living into the power of sin, Paul wants the lives of the early Christians to reflect the power of God's transforming love. In doing so, their story of faith would begin and end in a way that glorifies God. The beginning, middle, and end of the early Christians' faith journey is important to Paul.

Just as there are three different versions of *Little Shop of Horrors*, there are also three different versions of the story's ending. The one that intrigues me the most is the ending originally intended for the Frank Oz version from 1986. In this version, Audrey II grows large enough to physically fight Seymour and eventually eats both him and Audrey. After digesting their blood, the plant then grows large enough to break free from its pot at the flower shop.

After leaving the shop, Audrey II travels across the Brooklyn Bridge, eats a subway train, and destroys a theater. At the same time—and unbeknownst to the audience—earlier in the movie an ancillary character has harvested leaves from the plant and begun to grow more versions of Audrey II. These new Audrey plants have been sold throughout America and eventually bloom and grow into new versions of Audrey II before attacking humans and overtaking the country.

Theatergoers did not like this ending, so Oz changed it to be more palatable. In the theatrical release, the movie ends with Seymour killing the plant and living happily ever after with Audrey, the woman of his dreams. In all three versions of *Little Shop of Horrors*, the plant's growth and massive size become a symbol of the control the plant has over Seymour's life. This focus on the ever-expanding size of the plant each time Seymour gives in to its wishes makes me think of the increasing potential for sin as we give in to our desires.

In Romans 12, it seems that Paul is imploring us to be careful about what we feed (what we give our time, energy, or attention to) because it may become a consuming force that overwhelms us, and every time we give into this force, the larger it grows and the more power it exhibits over our lives. Instead of feeding sin, we should feed God and transform our lives and the lives of others through love. One of the biggest challenges of being transformed by love is that while it is easy to fall into sin, living in love takes effort.

Living in love does not usually occur in the perfect environment: Love typically grows in uncomfortable circumstances. Love is developed by working through conflict with someone who has hurt you. Love is nurtured by allowing another person to have their way while you wait your turn. Love is made perfect through sacrifice. Love is made mature by not having to come out on top all the time. May we learn to love sacrificially so that God's desires for people and creation may be seen through us.

GO AND TELL THAT

Hairspray
1 Corinthians 12:12-14

Debuting as a successful film in 1988, then as a Tony Award-winning musical in 2002, and again as another successful film in 2007, the story of *Hairspray* takes place in Baltimore, Maryland, in 1962. It revolves around the blossoming relationships that form among high school students who are drastically different from each other and who society and their parents think should not mix.

The main character is Tracy Turnblad, who confidently describes herself as "pleasantly plump." Tracy loves to dance, and her dream is to appear on the popular teen dance show *The Corny Collins Show*. Although Tracy believes in herself, society looks down on her because she is plump like her mother. Tracy comes from a solidly middle-class family. Her best friend is the shy but cute Penny Pingleton, who comes from an interesting home. Her mother is in equal parts religious and racist. It does not take long before Penny's growing personality, her desire for independence, and her willingness to dance with Black students—which eventually leads to her attraction to a Black boy—become an issue.

Every teen-angst musical needs a young heartthrob, and Link Larkin fits that bill. Link is a popular white kid who tries to dance like the Black students from his school. Other students, both Black and white, look up to him because he is good-looking, has a larger-than-life personality, and is well connected. These qualities lead him to becoming one of the star dancers on *The Corny Collins Show*. The cast of characters is rounded out by Seaweed, a young Black male who is somewhat of a rebel. He is confident in himself and is not afraid to let people know he feels that he is equal to white people. He wants the opportunity to show the world that he, and people who look like him and live in his neighborhood, are just as valuable and capable as any white person.

The primary theme of *Hairspray* is that all people are worthy of being treated equally regardless of their circumstances, and that given the chance, anyone can make a positive contribution to their community.

Tracy is not attractive in a traditional sense, but she eventually begins to believe in herself. She also makes it her personal goal to spend more time with the Black students. As she grows in confidence, she begins a relationship with Link, the heartthrob, and leads a movement to integrate the segregated *Corny Collins Show*. Link had previously dated a traditionally pretty and upwardly mobile girl whose mother worked for the station that broadcasts *The Corny Collins Show*. As Link's eyes open to the beauty in Tracy, he becomes less concerned about keeping up appearances and begins to date her and spend time with Black students. Penny, who had previously led a sheltered life, finds freedom in dancing and falling in love with Seaweed.

Although race plays an important part in *Hairspray*, the musical is also about how people from different neighborhoods and social classes, people who are different sizes and shapes, and people who are good at different styles of dancing each bring something unique and beneficial to humanity. In 1 Corinthians 12:12-14, Paul talks to his readers about this. (Okay, so he does not specifically mention dancing to the church at Corinth, but I can hope that it was in the back of his mind!)

Paul writes 1 Corinthians to a congregation that is experiencing many of the same challenges brought up in *Hairspray*. Corinth is an important cosmopolitan city. People from different walks of life make their homes there because it is a place of opportunity. Not only is the city diverse, but the church at Corinth is also made up of very different people. They are diverse in terms of age, gender, ethnicity, political outlook, and social standing.

This diversity brings with it a certain level of distrust as the church members do not fully trust each other or play well together. For example, one member of the congregation, Crispus, had previously been a leader of a local

Jewish synagogue but is now a follower of Jesus. What kinds of tensions could arise from his participation in this congregation, and how different is this new community than the one he led previously?

Another member, Erastus, is the city treasurer. Can you think of any conflicts that may have arisen between him, a politically and economically well-to-do person and some of the lower-income members of the community such as slaves?

Not only do the church members come from different life circumstances, but each one also comes with a different talent, desire, and focus. Paul recognizes that one of the main challenges this group faces is how to respect and affirm the diversity in the group while also honoring their common calling. One of the underlying tensions within the congregation, and the city of Corinth, was a belief in hierarchy.

Rome is the world leader, the most powerful nation on earth. Its influence can be felt in every city, town, and village. The Roman emperor is thought to be a son of the gods, endowed with their power and authority. Everyone in the kingdom works to please the emperor, and this hierarchical mindset trickles down from the emperor to his subordinates, to their subordinates, and so on. Common people also adopt this mindset. In families, fathers are more important than mothers, who are more important than children. Even in the church, some people are more equal or more valuable than others—and this is the situation at the church in Corinth.

To combat this mindset, Paul uses the human body as the model for how diverse individuals can function within a local congregation and within the church at large. The analogy he uses is simple but powerful: The body is made up of many different parts, some of which are perceived as being more important than others. The truth, however, is that all parts serve a particular function. Although our legs and feet get the credit for our ability to walk, if our inner ear does not function correctly, we may experience dizziness so severe that we are unable to stand.

Or, if the smallest disk in our back is compressed, our legs may experience numbness and be unable to walk. Walking takes more than just healthy legs and feet; it takes multiple unseen parts of our body to be healthy and functioning correctly so that we can do the things we take for granted.

Paul is trying to convey that no one person in the body of Christ is insignificant—whether young or old, a seasoned believer or someone who has just placed their faith in Jesus, a female, or a person from a lower social class.

Everyone who claims faith in Jesus is important to God and to the local fellowship to which they belong. There is no hierarchy in God's eyes; everyone is on an equal footing. Brian Peterson writes that, "The end result of the body metaphor in Paul's hands is not the same old hierarchy, or even the inverse of that culturally expected pattern of domination with new people placed on the top, but a deep unity of the whole body, with each part cared for by the others."[1] All members are to recognize the value of others and to affirm their participation in the life of the body.

One of the most impactful songs of the *Hairspray* musical is a number titled "Run and Tell That," sung by Seaweed. As previously mentioned, Seaweed wants other people to recognize the beauty and value that Black culture brings to the community. He and his friends are tired of being treated as outsiders. They believe that if they are given a chance, the white students will see the value of their abilities and life experiences.

The phrase, "run and tell that," is typically associated with Black culture and struggle and carries the idea that a person will no longer take the abuse or marginalization that has been heaped upon them. This is true in *Hairspray*. Seaweed and his friends are regularly treated unjustly by their teachers and fellow students simply because of their skin color and the community in which they live. They live in a clear hierarchy and are prepared to push back against it.

But they are not alone. Tracy also lives within the hierarchy of what people think is beautiful. Because she is plump, she is not taken seriously, and no one ever expects her to fall in love with the cutest and most popular boy in school. Through her actions and those of Seaweed, integration becomes a reality.

When acceptance of uniquely-made people occurs within a congregation, Peterson calls it "holy diversity":

We often confuse unity with uniformity, because it is much easier to gather with people who are like ourselves than it is to reach across the divisions which mark our culture.

Since the church is intended to be a foretaste of the final reconciliation of all things that God promises, Paul calls the church to start acting that way. Thus, diversity within the church is not a problem to be avoided, solved, or managed, but a gift of God's grace and a sign of the Spirit at work.[2]

May we recognize and celebrate the holy diversity that is found within the communities in which God has placed us.

Notes

1 Brian Peterson, "Commentary on 1 Corinthians 12:12-31a," https://www.workingpreacher.org/commentaries/revised-common-lectionary/third-sunday-after-epiphany-3/commentary-on-1-corinthians-1212-31a-3 (accessed February 20, 2021).

2 Ibid.

LOVE IS HEALTHY

The Phantom of the Opera
1 Corinthians 13:1-8, 13

Written by the successful French crime novelist Gaston Leroux, *The Phanton of the Opera* first appeared in novel form in 1910. Although Leroux was already an established fiction writer at the time of the novel's publication, his reputation was further cemented through *Phantom*. The novel was successfully interpreted in movie form multiple times before Andrew Lloyd Webber re-envisioned it as a musical in 1986. Webber's vision has proved to be one of the most enduring and celebrated productions in the history of Broadway. After it was staged in London in 1986 and again on Broadway in 1988, *Phantom* was nominated for every major theater award, winning most of them.

At its core, *The Phantom of the Opera* is about love—needed love, hoped-for love, lost-and-found love, requited and unrequited love. This requited and unrequited love is best understood through the lives and relationships of the story's three main characters: Erik, Christine, and Raoul. The first character, Erik, is the Phantom of the Opera. He is also referred to as the Angel of the Opera. Due to his physical birth defect, Erik has not experienced either personal love or love from the community. He was described at birth as appearing corpse-like and resembling a living skull.

Since I am an Eighties baby, I imagine that Erik looked like a version of Skeletor from the *He-Man* cartoon series. In subsequent movies and the musical, this deformity covers half of his face, making him look like participant in a circus freak show. Because of this deformity, Erik has missed out on love because everyone—including his mother—is repulsed by his looks. In the novel, Erik makes up for this lack of love by traveling to foreign lands as a circus performer and builder of trick palaces.

He also learns construction and engineering, and from his well-rounded experiences he begins to create physical and musical masterpieces that culminate in the bowels of the Paris Opera House. While living below the opera house, Erik finds love in the voice of a young soprano named Christine. He is enthralled with her talent and looks but knows that she would be repulsed by his appearance. So, he forms a relationship with her by whispering compliments and advice through the walls of her dressing room.

Christine is a young singer who is hoping for an opportunity to show the world how much she loves singing opera. However, she has been overshadowed by another singer who does not have her talent. Although she has not received love from those who run the opera house, she finds the compliments and attention she seeks from the angelic voice behind the walls of her dressing room. That voice of the Angel of the Opera affirms Christine's talents and dreams. Over time she begins to feel love for this angel, but wonders how she could fall in love with someone she has never actually seen.

As fate would have it, a long-forgotten friend reappears in Christine's life, giving her a glimpse of what true love should look like. That friend is Raoul, whom she has not seen since her childhood. Christine has never thought of Raoul as anything but a friend, but Raoul has nurtured a crush on Christine since they were children. Now, however, they are no longer children: Christine is a blossoming opera star, and Raoul is a handsome and successful man. As an adult, he finally has the opportunity to be with the woman he has loved for so long. Raoul eventually proposes marriage, and Christine accepts. Everyone is happy—everyone except the angelic voice behind the dressing room walls. In jealousy and anger, a deformed version of love, the Phantom sets a plan in motion to destroy Christine, Raoul, and the opera. If he cannot have her, no one will.

As I mentioned earlier, love is at the heart of *The Phantom of the Opera*, especially requited and unrequited love on a personal and community level. Erik wants love from his family and community, but his deformity makes him unlovable, and the love he is able to experience through his relationship with Christine is deformed because it is based on jealously and the need for control. Christine wants love from her community, but it is elusive because other people overlook her talents. Raoul wants love from Christine, and he is willing to wait to receive it. Although love is prominent in this story, the love displayed is not always healthy.

In 1 Corinthians 13, Paul takes the time to explain to the church at Corinth what healthy love should look like. There is irony in Paul's words because we typically think of the verses in 1 Corinthians 13 as applying primarily to the love between two individuals. I, too, am guilty of this: I read this passage at a wedding ceremony I performed. While the bride and groom appreciated and affirmed Paul's words, the passage is not primarily about the love between a husband and wife.

As we read this passage in context, we begin to understand that Paul is not talking about individual love. He is writing to members of a community that is having trouble getting along with each other. Although Paul's words do apply to individuals in personal relationships, they first apply to the communities such individuals occupy. Paul explains that love for the whole community—not just for the individuals in that community—is where the power and responsibility in a community come from.

One of the reasons Paul has to address the subject of healthy love is because the church at Corinth is made up of very different people. They are diverse in terms of age, gender, ethnicity, political outlook, and social standing and do not fully trust each other. Paul writes the letter to address these types of tensions and to help members learn the skills they need to navigate the challenges that come from these types of relationships. Paul tells church members that healthy love for the community is the key to making it all work.

He also tells them what healthy love does and does not look like. Healthy love is patient with others; it acts kindly toward others; is not jealous of others; does not brag on itself; is not proud of itself; does not act in inappropriate ways toward others; does not desire things for itself above things that would benefit others; and does not get upset with others easily.

Instead, healthy love rejoices when other people rejoice; it is willing to help others bear their burdens; it believes in others and hopes on the behalf of others; it endures the trials and tribulations that come with being in relationship with other people without keeping tabs on how many times someone has done them wrong. Love, the kind that is sacrificial and accommodating of the needs of others, the kind that God expects and is influenced by the sacrifice of Jesus, is unfortunately lacking at the church in Corinth.

The characters in *The Phantom of the Opera* also struggle with this expectation of love. Erik's understanding of love is fractured because his mother and his community have failed to give him the healthy love he needs and craves. This has left a tremendous void in his life that he is trying to fill with Christine. Unfortunately, his love for Christine is based upon his desire to control her and make up for something that is missing in his own life.

Christine's understanding of love is also fractured because she is seeking the approval of others in an opera community that has not yet accepted her and fails to recognize her gifts. She fills the gap with the unhealthy attention of Erik, which ultimately leads to the near-death of Raoul, the one person who loves Christine sincerely. Raoul's love is not necessarily sacrificial, but it is true. As Christine begins to better understand Raoul's love for her, her love for him is transformed into a sacrificial love that fights to keep him alive. In the end, though, no one really wins.

Although *Phantom* is fictional, I cannot help but think how the characters' lives would have turned out differently if their communities had loved them adequately. If Erik's mother and the people Erik came in contact with would have looked past his external scars to see the creativity in his heart, he could have used the skills and talents he developed during his travels to create meaningful art and architecture instead of plotting to harm others. If Christine's community had loved her and recognized her talents, she would not have had to look for acceptance from a strange voice behind a wall.

How many lives in our communities are affected like those of Erik and Christine? How many times have we looked at people's scars first instead of looking into their hearts? How many times have we missed opportunities to recognize and celebrate others? How often have we missed opportunities to love others as we have been loved? How could Paul's understanding and practice of loving others, no matter how different they are from ourselves, affect the communities we live in?

— LOVE IS HEALTHY —

In light of all that continues to occur in our world, country, and communities, I pray that we continue to think about love's implications in our lives and the lives of others and to actively seek out opportunities to put Paul's principles into practice.

HARMONY
AMID
REAL LIFE

Mary Poppins
Philippians 2:1-11

The musical *Mary Poppins* traces back to a series of books by Australian-English writer P.L. Travers before being made into a movie by Walt Disney in 1964. Travers published the first *Mary Poppins* book in 1934 and the last in 1988, for a total of eight books. The book series was extremely popular with readers of all ages and explored the relationship between Mary Poppins, an English nanny with magical powers, and the Banks family who lived at Number 17 Cherry Tree Lane in London. As the series progressed, Mary Poppins' relationship with the family grew and changed based on the needs of the children. Although the series is named after Mary Poppins, the members of the fictional Banks family were interesting in their own way.

In the books, the father George Banks is employed by a bank. Mr. Banks is always busy—too busy, in fact, to have a meaningful relationship with his wife and five children. He spends most of his time working and attempting to appear as though he has his life under control. Mrs. Banks, who is named Winifred in the musical, is also very busy trying to figure out her purpose in life. In the books, Mrs. Banks is a stay-at-home mother who needs help raising her growing family. In the Disney movie musical, she is a suffragette who is too busy to give her children the attention they need. In the subsequent Broadway musical, Mrs. Banks is a former entertainment star trying to find her purpose in life after not having performed for several years.

The main problem facing the Banks family is that the family and those around them are not really getting along. With the challenges of managing their own lives, Mr. and Mrs. Banks are not treating each other as loving couples should, and they are not as focused on their children as they should be. With their parents preoccupied, the children are expected to act less like children and more like adults.

After several different nannies are unable to manage the two precocious older children, Mary Poppins is blown into their lives by a strong east wind. Through magical adventures and a spunky attitude, Mary Poppins helps the family transform into a more loving unit.

As an interesting side note, I discovered while researching the history of Mary Poppins that the popularity of the book series led to a number of companies offering to make Mary Poppins into a movie. Travers hated the idea of the books being made into a movie, and for years refused every offer—even from Walt Disney, whose daughters loved the books. It took almost twenty years and multiple offers before Travers finally agreed to allow Disney to produce Mary Poppins for the big screen.

As Disney anticipated, the movie was a box office success and received thirteen Academy Award nominations, eventually winning four, including Best Film Editing, Best Original Music Score, Best Song (for "Chim-Chim-Cher-ee") and Best Actress (for Julie Andrews). Unfortunately, Travers hated the movie, so much so that she refused to allow Disney to make a follow-up picture. In addition, she almost refused to allow her characters to be reimagined for Broadway. She eventually allowed a musical to be written and produced, but her caveat was that no one who had worked on the Disney movie would be allowed to contribute to a new Broadway musical.

Thinking through *Mary Poppins*, it appears that the primary, underlying theme of the story is that a person's life will be affected based on how that life is lived. Thus, a positive attitude about life will lead to a positive outcome in life. A hardworking attitude toward life will lead to a productive and beneficial life. However, there is a secondary theme: having an open attitude toward people who are different than us can lead to unexpected experiences and friendships that benefit everyone. This seems to be the point of the song "Chim-Chim-Cher-ee," one of the more popular songs from the musical and movie.

"Chim-Chim-Cher-ee" shares the idea that people should not judge a book by its cover. A gruff, dirty chimney sweep may be the happiest person you will ever meet, and your life may be changed for the better if you do not judge them by their looks or their occupation and instead welcome them into your life. This same idea is at the core of Philippians 2 where Paul encourages his readers to view each other in a better light by welcoming the opportunity to see each other as God sees them and enjoying the positive impact they can make in each other's lives.

Throughout history, Rome founded smaller colonies on the outer rings of its ever-expanding empire to keep the peace among its citizens and to guard against invasions from external, barbaric hordes. The colonies that Rome most appreciated were those that were loyal to the Roman way of life. Philippi was one such city, a proud colony famous for being a miniature Rome: In Philippi, citizens followed Roman protocols with pride. Philippians spoke the Roman language, used Roman titles, followed Roman customs, managed their affairs according to Roman practice, and dressed as Rome dictated.

For the most part, residents of Philippi rejected the influence of the world around them in favor of making Rome happy. However, within the city, a small group of Christ-followers popped up who attempted to live from a foundation different than Rome's. Just imagine the challenges that must have arisen given that most people in the city followed Caesar when this small group of people gave their allegiance to Jesus!

One of the reasons Paul wrote to the church at Philippi was to encourage its worshipers as they experienced the tensions that came from having a different allegiance than most people in that city. Knowing there would be challenges in worshiping a god other than Caesar, Paul wants believers to maintain their faith, even as it becomes a social and political struggle. According to Paul, believers are not to hide or apologize for who they are or how they choose to live. Paul knows this will not be easy because following Jesus will require believers to say "no" to Rome and Caesar while saying "yes" to Jesus.

In chapter 2, Paul also reaches out to this small group of believers because he knows they need to be encouraged not to turn against each other when times become hard and their faith brings the potential for persecution.

After all, what typically happens when life does not go the way we anticipate, or takes an unexpected turn, or the pressures ramp up? We are sometimes tempted to turn against those whom we love and live with in community.

For example, when our nation began to feel the full force of the Covid-19 pandemic and people were laid off from work, lawyers reported a drastic increase in divorce inquiries and filings due to people being unable to handle the pressure of such impactful life changes and, instead, taking out their frustrations on those they loved. Counselors and mental health professionals reported similar spikes in family conflicts due to the impact of the pandemic.

Similarly, the church at Philippi was experiencing an external problem leading to internal conflict. In the letter to the Philippians, Paul references some type of previously occurring conflict but never fully explains or identifies what it is. He acknowledges that the conflict has begun to divide the group, and he encourages members of the group to see each other not as adversaries or enemies but as co-laborers and family members who not only shared a common Savior but also a common calling and purpose.

This camaraderie could be difficult to maintain, especially due to the diversity present in the Philippian congregation—a cosmopolitan body made up of Jews, Gentiles, and others who had come to the city to improve their fortunes. Members of the group brought with them their individual histories, cultures, and belief systems, all of which were influenced by the words and works of Jesus and each other. When you add this to the social and political pressures believers were already experiencing, it is understandable why the group was fracturing.

Paul is determined to help believers overcome their challenges and stay together as a cohesive group. He challenges them to treat each other in the ways that God wants and to conduct themselves in a manner worthy of the name of Christ. He wants them to be of the same mind and have the same attitude about life and living together. I do not believe that he is asking them to agree on everything or to give up their individuality. Instead, I think he is asking them to have a common attitude and orientation toward each other and life so that they would not turn against each other but would stand together and live in a way that exemplifies the teachings of Jesus.

This was also part of Mary Poppins' purpose in visiting the Banks family at 17 Cherry Tree Lane. The Banks family is experiencing stress that is causing them to not see each other in the ways they should. They have forgotten they are family: Mr. Banks, in particular, has forgotten this. But thanks to Mary Poppins and a motley crew of characters, the Banks family is brought back together in love (in under two hours!).

If only real life were like that! How much easier would it be if we could anticipate a nanny being blown into our lives by a strong wind and a magical umbrella, with catchy show tunes and cute animated friends to boot, who tells us when we are getting things right or wrong and who uses a spoonful of sugar to conquer our challenges?

We all know that is not real life. When life goes wrong, all we have is each other. Well, each other, God's word, and the commitments we have made to each other—commitments to love each other, walk with each other, serve with each other, protect each other, encourage each other, and be patient with each other. Paul's words are as relevant to us as they were to the believers in Philippi. May we be found caring for each other and treating each other in ways that are pleasing to God.

WHERE'S YOUR YELLOW TICKET?

Les Misérables
James 2:1-9

The musical *Les Misérables* is based on the 1862 novel of the same name written by Victor Hugo. *Les Misérables* takes place in France in the years 1815 to 1832 and is told through the eyes of several characters who are, for one reason or another, miserable. *Les Mis* is not a happy musical. In fact, it is one of the most depressing stories you may ever encounter. What makes it so depressing? It examines how the poor and socially outcast interact both with those who live in high society and other poor people. Three characters hold most of our attention: Jean Valjean, Javert, and Fantine.

Jean Valjean is a man caught stealing bread so he can provide food for his sister and her many children. For violating the sanctity of community, he is sentenced to five years hard labor on a chain gang. In prison, Jean Valjean witnesses how unkind humanity can be. Unwilling to live under such circumstances, he tries many times to escape his confinement, only to be caught repeatedly. Each time he is caught, more years are added to his sentence.

What starts as a five-year prison term balloons to nineteen years of separation from his family. The day finally comes when Jean Valjean is no longer physically imprisoned, but he also no longer resembles the man who entered prison many years earlier. He is changed, and not for the better. Jean Valjean is scarred physically, mentally, and emotionally and is facing the challenge of starting over.

Javert is the guard who works in the prison where Jean Valjean is held. Eventually, he too leaves the prison and becomes the director of a police department in a small town. Javert is not poor monetarily, but he experiences a severe deficiency when it comes to showing compassion for others. Javert is a police officer who does everything by the book. Unfortunately, his book does not have a chapter titled "compassion."

Javert is a stickler for doing what is "right" or what is lawful. If it is not lawful, he will not let anyone get away with it, regardless of circumstances. If a crime is committed, it must be punished. If an infraction occurs, it must be addressed. The irony is that Javert legitimately believes he is doing the right thing by being so rigid in his application of the law. He wholeheartedly believes in two things: God and the law, and not necessarily in that order. And in his mind, neither of them is merciful.

The third main character is Fantine, a female factory worker who has previously enjoyed an illicit sexual relationship with a socially prominent man. Unfortunately for Fantine, she becomes pregnant and her secret lover leaves her high and dry. Uneducated, unmarried, and penniless, this single mother is the definition of poor and outcast. To maintain hope for a better future, she decides to leave her child in the custody of another family while she seeks work. She eventually secures a job at a local factory and uses her earnings to pay the family to continue raising her child.

Fantine keeps her job until she rebuffs the sexual advances of her supervisor. In shame and anger, this man waits for his opportunity to exact revenge. Eventually, he finds his opportunity after several men in the factory find out about Fantine's illegitimate child. He uses this newfound knowledge as the basis to fire her. Without a job, Fantine is forced to make money any way she can, first, selling her two front teeth, then her hair, and finally, her body.

Throughout *Les Misérables*, we follow characters who struggle because of their stations in life. Small mistakes bring about big consequences, followed by years of tension and pain. Careless decisions carry grave consequences. And worst of all, we see people repeatedly not treating each other well. Mistreatment of others is a hallmark of this story. In addition, a theme that runs through the story is the idea of "pursuit": Someone, or something, is either pursuing someone else or being pursued themselves.

Jean Valjean is initially pursued by the baker from whom he stole the bread to feed his family. He is then pursued and caught by the police. After going to prison, Jean Valjean is in constant pursuit of freedom. He yearns to sleep in a real bed, eat a home-cooked meal, and experience a decent shave. This pursuit of freedom leads him to try to escape multiple times, each time being pursued by Javert and the other guards.

Eventually Jean Valjean leaves prison for good, but it appears that he will be forever pursued by his past. Everywhere he goes, his sin is staring him in the face. Sometimes his sin takes on a unique form. For example, after Jean Valjean obtains his freedom from prison, he is required to carry and display a yellow "ticket of leave" at all times. This yellow ticket brands him as a former prisoner and as someone who is untrustworthy, vile, and an outcast.

All the years of suffering for Jean Valjean are personified in that small yellow piece of paper. His past will forever cast a shadow over him that he cannot escape. Even after Jean Valjean moves to another town under an assumed name and becomes both a wealthy businessman and the town mayor, his past continues to pursue him. Javert, the by-the-book prison guard, becomes the lead police officer in that town, and the cycle of Javert pursuing Valjean to punish him for his past starts again.

Jean Valjean is not the only person being pursued by their past. Fantine, the single, unwed mother from the factory is also being pursued. Every day she is chased by the memory of the relationship that produced her daughter. She cannot get away from the repercussions of being poor and raising a child as a single mother or from the stigma that it encourages. Her coworkers expect that she will be open and accepting of their sexual advances toward her because they view her as an object. After she is fired from her job, she cannot find another, and her life spirals downward until one day a man insults her and tries to take physical advantage of her. When she defends herself, she is arrested by Javert, and we know that he will not have any mercy upon her.

Jean Valjean and Fantine are not the only characters being pursued. Javert is also a man on the run. He, too, is running from his past—his father was a prison convict, and his mother was an imprisoned gypsy who gave birth to him while incarcerated. Ironically, the prison where Javert was born is the same prison where he works and that holds Jean Valjean. Because of the pain and shame Javert feels about his pedigree, he renounces his parents and becomes a guard in the prison in which he was born. He is dogged by his less-than-honorable beginnings and cannot rest unless he is doing something meaningful with his life. For Javert, that "something" is to become the embodiment of justice.

The struggles, fears, and themes of the musical, especially the idea of how not to treat the poor, are also found in James 2. The church to which James writes is made up of Gentiles and other followers converted from Judaism. Within this diverse group there is a certain level of social tension, which includes the place of the poor. It is a common belief that a person could become poor or have a lower social status due to personal decisions or sin. If a person were poor due to personal decisions, they would be treated as a second-class citizen.

Sometimes, the people who hold to this belief system fail to recognize that a person can be poor not because of something they have done, but because of something someone else has done that affects them. If a woman finds herself to be struggling because her husband has died, it is difficult for her to make a living. If a family's land catches on fire and their crops are destroyed, the family could lose everything they own. If a boy's sheep are stolen, he could be left with no income.

Being poor brings with it segregation. Although it seems that most members of the congregation James writes to are not wealthy, James recognizes that there is still the potential for some of them to make a public distinction between the rich and poor, the socially acceptable and unacceptable. If a person from a higher social position comes into the meeting space wearing expensive clothes or fancy jewelry, that person would be treated like royalty. They would also be given the best seat in the building.

But, if a person comes in who occupies a lower social rung, there is the potential for them to be treated poorly. Instead of being offered a seat of comfort, they might be told to sit on the floor like a servant or slave. Because they do not have the proper social status, such people could be treated as "other" and not equals. James describes this process as "showing partiality." The New Testament church had to deal with the same issues of Victor Hugo's day.

James tells the members of the church that God condemns their actions of partiality because God does not value material riches, political positions, or social status above people. Instead, God values the poor, the downtrodden, and those who have excessive spiritual riches. Instead of giving people respect based on their possessions or social status, church members are encouraged to love all people equally, recognizing that regardless of their station in life, all people are created by God and embody God's image. In God's eyes, the miserable deserve as much love and respect as the rich or socially affluent.

Although *Les Misérables* is a fictional story, the points it makes still ring true today, and although James wrote his letter to believers hundreds of years ago, his words retain a sense of freshness that is still relevant today. Some of us hold to the mindset that people who find themselves in difficult positions in life are there simply because of the bad decisions they have made; we may believe that their lives are not as good as ours because of what they have done to themselves—and we may be right in our assumptions. They may well have made bad choices that have taken them down the path of no return, but I am willing to bet that all of us have made questionable decisions sometime in our lives.

We should remember the adage, "There but for the grace of God go I." The difference between our situation and the life of a poor person has been God's grace. That grace may have taken the form of loving parents who supported us and helped us during times of need, or as good friends who watched over us. When we see someone of a lower social status than us, we cannot dismiss them as being merely products of their own decisions. People are the creations of God, no matter how broken or lost they may be, and God wants them to experience the same grace that we ourselves have experienced. We are the vessels for that grace to be poured into their lives.

We are commanded by God to love all people equally. When someone who is "other" approaches us, we must interact with them as Christ would, regardless of their geography, nationality, race, political standing, or attire. We should see them through the eyes of Christ, and they should see Christ looking back at them through our actions.

We must ask ourselves: Will we treat interactions with the "least of these" as an opportunity to exhibit the gifts of the Spirit and live out our faith in tangible ways, or will we simply go through the motions?

CONCLUSION
The Gospel Revisited

Some readers may not understand why this book is titled *The Gospel According to Broadway*, particularly when most of the chapters do not explicitly share the gospel in a way that is traditionally evangelical. According to U.S. evangelicals, the gospel is solely about God's displeasure with humankind due to human sin and humanity's need to assuage God's anger in order to be forgiven and enter heaven upon earthly death.

The only thing that could appease God's anger was for God to send Jesus, the holy and righteous Son, to die on the cross and provide an adequate sacrifice to atone for humanity's sins. (Think about the sacrificial lamb and the Day of Atonement from the Introduction.) According to this view, Jesus' death, burial, and resurrection are the most important occurrences in history, and these sacrificial acts should be the focus of our relationship with God and with each other. Life with God is about being forgiven of sin and going to heaven. Life with each other is about helping people learn that they need to be saved and telling them how to experience personal salvation.

However, in my opinion, this is only a partial interpretation of the gospel. If we look at the totality of the Bible, the gospel is the story of God's love for creation and humankind and God's desire to be in relationship with everything and everyone. When God created all things, life was how God wanted it to be. When God created humankind, the world was good until the point at which humankind did the opposite of what God wanted. This action and attitude caused God's relationship with humankind and creation to change.

God held humankind accountable for this change but did not end the relationship. Instead, God reaffirmed God's desire to remain in relationship with humankind. This desire was fully understood through God's relationship with a particular family—the family of Abraham. God determined that through Abraham's family, God would not only repair and reestablish relationships with one family, but with all families to come.

In the overall story, humankind as represented by the family of Abraham did not fully appreciate what God was attempting to do on their behalf. Time and again, Abraham's descendants failed to honor the relationship God was trying to establish with them. They either forgot what God wanted for and from them, or they outright ignored God's desires. Accordingly, God allowed them to experience the consequences of their actions.

As I briefly mentioned in the Preface, most good stories have a transition. After the author has explained the characters, setting, plot, and conflict, he or she begins to reveal how the conflict will be resolved. I think the resolution to the conflict that has been inherent in God's relationship with humankind is revealed in the writings of Isaiah. Although God allows humankind to experience the consequences of our actions, God promises us that that we will never be fully removed from God's love and will; eventually, we will experience full redemption and restoration.

Several themes run through Isaiah's writings, namely hope, joy, and peace. These three themes find their completion in the larger idea of what people can experience by knowing that God loves them. According to Isaiah, these themes would find their fulfillment in the birth of someone sent specifically by God to provide followers full restoration to relationship with God.

This idea of a savior being born is not unique to Isaiah. There are many places in the scriptures of Israel where the story of the birth of someone important to God's people is relayed through prophecies and anticipated by God's children. Isaiah 9:2-7 speaks of One who would come and do something wonderful on God's behalf for God's children. This passage is about the hope, joy, and peace that God would deliver to a people through a new leader born for their sake.

Depending on which verses of Isaiah you read, this act would either happen in the future, or it has already happened. Whether it is about to

— CONCLUSION —

occur or has already occurred, this action is the result of God's immeasurable love for God's people and God's desire to fulfill God's promises to cherish and protect the world. Through the birth of this new leader, the lives of God's people would change from despair to ones filled with hope, joy, and peace.

This idea is found is Isaiah 9, which I must admit does not initially feel like a passage of hope, joy, or peace. God's people are in an extremely difficult position: The nation of Judah has already experienced an attack by a military enemy aided by Judah's cousin, the nation of Israel. This attack occurs because the king of Judah, King Ahaz, has ignored Isaiah's council about a military coalition, which means that he is ignoring God's council. The king's disregard for what God has said through Isaiah leads to the kingdom being attacked, people being taken as prisoners of war, and fear running rampant. King Ahaz, however, is not the only person who disregards God's will.

The book of Isaiah is filled with prophecies that originate from God's displeasure with the sins of humankind, including people's disregard of God's wishes for how they should live and treat others. The people of Judah regularly disregard God's will, leading to stern prophecies and a certain despair that hovers over the book. There is also a uniqueness about Isaiah in that it is not a linear book. Some of the prophecies are out of sequence, and there is not necessarily a cause that leads to an effect. There are points in Isaiah where a future response is predicted in response to a past action. In other places, a current event is the response to a past action or a current event is predicated on God's knowing how people will act in the future.

The book of Isaiah begins with God pronouncing judgment against the people of Judah because of their wickedness. It then tells the story of how, despite the land and people of Judah being corrupted and harmed, God would eventually restore both to their intended purpose. The prophecies of Isaiah move back and forth between describing how God's people would be punished for their sinfulness and how they could still hope for their future restoration. God would not hold their rebellion against them forever but would, instead, forgive and restore both the people and their land to their rightful places.

Isaiah also prophesies a time of exile in a foreign land and the joys the people would experience when they emerged from that exile. The dismay they would feel seeing their homeland overrun by a foreign power would not compare to the joy of returning home and starting their lives over.

Although the people of Judah would become subject to a foreign ruler, God would send someone to return them to their former glory as a people and a nation. In Isaiah 9, the writer tells God's people that although God has passed judgment against them for their sins, God would eventually send someone who would change their fortunes for the better. This new leader would be different from the types of kings the people were used to following. He would be faithful to his calling to lead God's people instead of using his royal position for personal gain. Whereas prior kings had served God half-heartedly and were concerned only about their personal stature, this new leader would put God first and would fully live into his call to protect and lead God's people. He would be better even than King David, who served as the gold standard for Hebrew kings. This would be a welcome change in leadership.

The new king would faithfully serve God and the people, and with his service would come transformation. The cloud of darkness under which the nation had lived would give way to God's glorious light. The people of Judah would no longer be victims at the hands of others. Instead, they would become victors over their enemies. They would experience freedom, restoration, and a return to their homeland. Isaiah's description of the leader God would send to bring about this change is replete with strong military language. This new king would lead the people to victory over their enemies, and the enemies would not simply be hurt—they would be crushed and their weapons destroyed.

Having been born in St. Louis, Missouri—the city where I currently reside—I think that a modern equivalent to Isaiah's prophecy might be for the Cardinals to get a new manager who is better than all the combined former Cardinal managers. After hiring the manager, the Cardinals would face the Kansas City Royals in the World Series. The Cardinals would not only sweep the Royals, but the Royals would not get a hit nor have anyone reach first base during the entire series. The only thing that could make things worse for the Royals would be for Cardinals fans to burn the Royals equipment van so the Royals would not have any gloves or bats to take home with them and for Cardinals fans to dance while they watch the van burn.

This is how decisive a victory God's children would experience with the new king. The primary challenge the original readers of this passage experienced was that this king did not arrive during the lifetime of the writer of Isaiah or of the people who most desperately needed and wanted the salvation being promised.

So, what does this mean for people like us who are disconnected by generations from the experiences of the writer and his audience? How can we understand this passage in the twenty-first century or apply it to what is currently happening in our world? I think the answer can be found in the example of what regularly occurs within Death Valley National Park.

Death Valley straddles portions of Nevada and California and is the second-largest national park in the United States. Its boundaries cover portions of the Great Basin in Nevada to the Mojave Desert in California, some of the harshest terrain found in the United States.

Death Valley has a reputation for being harsh and unforgiving. It is a place lacking in both beauty and compassion for anyone who attempts to enter it. The area is alleged to have received its name in 1849 from prospective gold miners who lost their way while traveling to California. After an unplanned, two-month, 120-mile trek through this barren wasteland, one of the last miners to find his way out said, "Goodbye, Death Valley," and the moniker stuck.

But something strange happens periodically in Death Valley: it transforms from dry, barren wasteland to fields of vibrant color. During a super bloom, Death Valley becomes a place of beauty and life. A super bloom is a natural phenomenon where places that do not typically harbor much life or color bring forth an abundance of it. Super blooms do not just happen, though. Special circumstances are needed for them to occur. In his book, *We Stood Upon Stars: Finding God in Lost Places*, Roger Thompson describes the circumstances necessary: First, seeds must somehow ride the winds to Death Valley and settle on the desert floor. Then, as Thompson explains:

> The desert must receive rainfall in the autumn, and this rain must penetrate deep into the soil matrix in order to reach a majority of the dormant seeds of flowering plants. If subsequent rainfall is excessive or inundating, the young plants may be carried away in flash floods; if it is inadequate, the seeds will die from dehydration.
>
> Next, the ground in which the seeds lie must warm slowly over the several months which follow the first soaking rain, and the desert must have enough cloud cover both to shield the soil from intense daytime desert heat and to insulate it from overnight freezing temperatures. Finally, once the newly germinated plants have reached the surface of the soil, the desert must remain undisturbed by strong winds which would uproot the plants or damage the young shoots. The rare concentration of these events is what makes a super bloom such an extraordinary occurrence.[1]

I see similarities between the super bloom in Death Valley and the words and promises we find in the writings of Isaiah. In Isaiah 35:1-10, the writer appears to be describing a physical and spiritual super bloom that will eventually occur for his intended audience.

The context of Isaiah 35 is one of waste and bareness—akin to a desert. The audience of Isaiah 35 is living under harsh physical and spiritual conditions. Because of their continual practice of forsaking God by mistreating their countrymen and those on the outskirts of society, God allows them to experience military defeat by a stronger foreign power, the Assyrians, that besieges Jerusalem and leave it in ruins. The Assyrians remove the leaders of God's people from the city in chains as the city burns and take them to a foreign land.

Those who are not taken are left in a city that can no longer provide for them. To add insult to injury, this military power also destroys the temple of God. Yet, seemingly out of nowhere, and amid the hopelessness and despair that God's people are experiencing from the fallout of this military defeat, the prophet of God gives them a message that all hope is not lost: the current circumstances will not last forever. Hope is on the way.

Up to this point, the book of Isaiah is filled with God's scolding words of judgment against the people of Judah. When the prophet is not speaking against the people, he is telling their captors that God will hold them accountable for their sins.

And then the words of chapter 35 appear. Isaiah 35 reads like the calm eye of a hurricane surrounding a peaceful island while the rest of the sea is

— CONCLUSION —

in turmoil. Here, the prophet tells the people of Judah that God is on the way to help them. God will heal their land, free their people, and eventually lead their captives home. Isaiah 35 outlines a series of things God will do for them that will not only restore their hope but will also reaffirm God's love for them.

First, God will restore their barren land to its former glory. Where there had been death, new life will grow. Crumbled walls will be rebuilt and will once again provide protection. Homes that had been burned will again become places where families break bread and share stories. Streets will bustle with business, and the city will have thriving commerce. Judah will once again be the envy of other nations. The people will no longer be ashamed of their homeland; instead, it will be a source of pride for them.

Not only will God restore the land, but God will also restore the people. God will heal their bodies: Those who are disabled or incomplete in society's eyes will be made whole. The blind will see, the lame will not only walk but will leap like deer. The people will experience both an individual and a communal super bloom.

This change will occur because God promises to take revenge against their enemies. God will not allow the Assyrians to remain in power; God will turn the tables and free God's people, allowing them to return home. Linda Day writes: "The original audience for this prophecy was those living under the oppression of foreign [Babylonian, then Persian, then Hellenistic] rule. Redemption in this context is freedom from political captivity, an actual physical release so that the people can imagine journeying back to Jerusalem."[2]

This redemption and return home would be facilitated by the physical fall of the captors. After the fall of their enemies, the people of Judah would be provided with a way to return home—and not just a way; God would provide them with a safe road to travel through the wilderness. The idea of wilderness was important to the people. The wilderness, much like Death Valley, was not a good place to find oneself, let alone travel through.

According to Isaiah, the journey through the wilderness would resemble the earlier time when God led their ancestors to the Promised Land. It would be a journey to freedom and restoration. Anathea Portier-Young writes that,

"Wilderness is where God's people learn to trust. In wilderness God carried them [their ancestors], fed them, and gave them improbable water. In wilderness God found God's people, guarded and cared for them, and lifted them up."[3]

The prophet says that God will do the same thing for this new generation. The words of hope that the prophet speaks are possible because God will rescue God's people. God has not forgotten about them. God will lead them to freedom and restoration.

These words of the prophet are ones that many of us need right now. Although God will allow us to endure temporary dry conditions, we will eventually experience the right conditions for a super bloom to occur. God will cause dry land to produce life. God will cause darkness and grayness to give way to light and color. God will allow hopelessness to be replaced by hope. Sooner rather than later, God will allow us to leave Babylon and return to Zion. In the words of Casey Thornburgh Sigmon, "Harsh, undesirable conditions ... seem to pave the way for the stunning explosion of a super bloom."[4]

Readers may wonder what any of this has to do with the gospel. I believe the gospel is the story of God's love for creation and God's efforts to be in relationship with creation. Since God has been willing to go to extreme lengths to forgive sin and restore humankind to its proper status in God's kingdom, we can have hope that nothing will separate us from God's love.

Sometimes encouraging words such as these may seem unrealistic, especially when we experience circumstances that are out of our control. I am hopeful that soon, COVID will be a distant memory. As I hope for that, however, I recognize that the effects of the pandemic may still be felt by millions of Americans who have lost loved ones, businesses, and other, less tangible things. A recovered economy will not bring back loved ones who died at the hands of an invisible enemy. In addition, this does not begin to address the long-term devastation experienced by poorer nations.

One of the challenges we now face is keeping our expectations realistic. With the vaccine being distributed and our nation generally moving in a positive direction, we may, with good reason, begin to dream big about life

— CONCLUSION —

again. While we should celebrate our victories, however, now is the time to remain grounded in God's faithfulness, which is present during both good and bad times. We can learn this by reading Isaiah 61:10–62:5.

As God promises through the prophet Isaiah, the people of Judah do eventually experience freedom. By the time we arrive at Isaiah 61 and 62, the people are no longer political prisoners nor living in a foreign land. They have returned home to the city of Jerusalem. But although they are free, the people of Judah are still experiencing challenges: Life is not as perfect as they had anticipated. Their city is not yet fully rebuilt, their homes are not restored, the Temple is not fully restored, the city's walls and protective gate are not fully restored, and the construction projects to accomplish the rebuilding have met with obstacles and delays.

In response to these delays, the people question God's love for them. People who had been filled with hope and thankfulness for gaining their long-awaited freedom are now experiencing frustration and pain because their anticipated freedom does not look as expected. Where there had previously been faith in God's power and thankfulness for it, there is now frustration and doubt. The people wonder if God is strong enough to fulfill the promises that had been made to them, and if God truly cares about them.

Have you experienced such a pendulum swing of emotions related to your faith in God? One moment things are not going well, but then a glimmer of hope pops up on the horizon and your faith swings in the other direction as God's power is restored. Then something goes wrong again, and you find yourself once again questioning God.

It is important for us to recognize these times in our lives. We should not act as though this does not happen. As important as it is to celebrate the uplifting moments in life when we can clearly see that God has come through for us, we should also feel free to acknowledge when it seems as though God is far away. It is one of the uneasy balancing acts of being in relationship with God and each other. W. Carter Lester writes, "Part of the power of the Bible is the good news it has to offer to people who desperately need to hear such news, but the other part of the Bible's power is its ability to name the reality that people are facing."[5]

In Isaiah 62, the writer identifies points of hope for the people's future. God's people will be changed for the better, and hope for their future will be reflected in new names that God will give them, names that other people will recognize and respect, names that most readers will already know are important in the scriptures of Israel. Lester continues:

> Names in the Old Testament offer clues to the character of the person named. A change in name can represent a change in character, such as the new name of Israel given to Jacob. Here in Isaiah 62, the name change does not just describe the change in Israel's character; it also describes the change in God's relationship with Israel and in Israel's future.[6]

Hope will be found in the new names bestowed upon the people by God. These names will also reflect the new purposes that are to be given by God. Ultimately, this is the hope that the writer of Isaiah 61 and 62 is sharing with readers: God has not forgotten about God's children. A delay in the arrival or completion of certain promises is not a denial of the future fulfillment of past promises.

I think we can all stand to be reminded of this truth: delays do not mean denials. God is saying this to an earlier generation of people who are dependent on holy intervention for their needs, but we today also can claim the same promise as true for our lives today. I say this knowing that sometimes it does not seem to be the case, but as the writer claims a brighter future for God's people, we can do the same for each other.

What we see before us is not all there is to life. Just as the prophet does, we too should trust that God is true to God's promises and that we can look forward to a joyful future based on these promises. This hope is the essence of the gospel. It moves us forward personally and communally. God's love overcomes the misfortune, pain, and tragedy of life, but the gospel is not just about the security of our souls after we die. Prior to that, it is about our relationship with our Creator and how that relationship impacts our relationships with others. This is what the gospel writers show us through the stories they share about Jesus' life and ministry.

I have two overall hopes for readers of this book: First, I hope you will be reminded that God's story is our story. It is our story because God invites

— CONCLUSION —

each of us to participate in it. This invitation is not based on who you are, where you grew up, or what you have or have not achieved in life; it is based on God's unwavering love for you and how you will receive this love. Second, I hope you will remember that God wants you to share that love with others and for others to share that love with you. God wants human relationships to experience restoration and to function as God intended before sin and mistrust entered the story.

God also wants this love as expressed through Jesus' resurrection to change individuals, communities, cities, countries, and the world through the hope that accompanies the incarnation of God's love through Jesus. As Carla Works writes, "When God reveals God's self, our little worlds are transformed. We cannot go on with life as normal, because we cannot un-see God in our midst. Like Paul, we are unworthy of this life-changing revelation. May we work tirelessly—as Paul did—to extend God's grace to others."[7]

The gospel is not only the story of what happened to Jesus centuries ago; it is also the story about who we can become because Jesus fulfilled God's wishes for reconciliation and restoration. The gospel is about how we can become resurrection people ourselves and how we can live into God's desires for love, community, forgiveness, and sacrifice for the sake of others. Amen.

Notes

1 Roger Thompson, *We Stood Upon Stars: Finding God in Lost Places* (New York: Crown Publishing Group, 2017), 160.

2 Linda Day, "The Politics of Isaiah 35:1-10," https://politicaltheology.com/the-politics-of-isaiah-351-10/ (accessed January 21, 2021).

3 Ibid.

4 Casey Thornburgh Sigmon, "Commentary on Isaiah 35:1-10," https://www.workingpreacher.org/commentaries/revised-common-lectionary/third-sunday-of-advent/commentary-on-isaiah-351-10-5 (accessed January 20, 2021).

5 W. Carter Lester, "Isaiah 62:1-5: Pastoral Perspective," in *Feasting on the Word: Preaching the Revised Common Lectionary*, Year C, vol. 1 (Louisville, KY: Westminster John Knox Press, 2009), 244.

6 Ibid.

7 Carla Works, "Commentary on 1 Corinthians 15:1-11," https://www.workingpreacher.org/commentaries/revised-common-lectionary/fifth-sunday-after-epiphany-3/commentary-on-1-corinthians-151-11-6 (accessed February 10, 2021).

www.ingramcontent.com/pod-product-compliance
Lightning Source LLC
Chambersburg PA
CBHW071009160426
43193CB00012B/1988